David Thomson

PERMISSION TO PHOTOCOPY

ACKNOWLEDGEMENTS

Firstly, I should like to acknowledge the on-going support of the staff and pupils of St John's College School, Cambridge, in the development of these materials.

Secondly, I should like to acknowledge the influence of the following people on my thinking: Steve Bowkett, Kevin Jones, Nancy Kline, Jenny Mosley (who inspired some of the circle games) and Simon Shaw; and Oliver Caviglioli, Ian Harris and Bill Tindall from Model Learning Ltd (from whom I have borrowed the ten circles game in Conversation 6). I should like to thank Tony Gregorc particularly for his support and insight on learning styles.

Thirdly, I should like to record my thanks to the following colleagues and friends for their suggestions on my early drafts: Matthew Benton, Katharine Boness, Ian Hunter, Emma Loveridge, Alison Morris, Helen and John Patrick, Debbie Pullinger and Mary Rycroft.

Fourthly, I should like to acknowledge the work and influence of Corin Redsell and the professionalism and guidance of the staff at LDA.

Finally, I want to acknowledge the invaluable support of my parents Gordon and Brown Thomson and my brothers Michael and George. A heartfelt thank you to Howard, Sarah, Lydia, Simeon, Dominic, Felix, Camilla, Aurelia, Pascale and Linus Chilvers for all you have taught me about learning.

For information about INSET and workshops that are run with staff, pupils and parents based on this work and other aspects of teaching and learning, please visit my website at www.futuremind.co.uk. Please contact me via RSG@futuremind.co.uk with your comments on these materials.

David Thomson, Cambridge, August 2006

CONTENTS

INTRODUCTION

This course is designed to help pupils in years 5-8 make friends with study. It facilitates teaching through structured conversations and taps into the power of reflective learning.

The vast majority of study skills textbooks are aimed at upper-secondary and college and university students (Hoffman 1999 and Hubbard 2000 are exceptions). *ReadyStudyGo!* aims to fill the gap in the materials available for younger students.

During this course, pupils will:

- become more self-aware as students;

- discover and develop their personal approach to study;

- learn to understand their peers better;

- learn to express what they think about school and school work from a personal perspective;

- improve their speaking and listening;

- boost their study self-esteem;

- develop more independence and responsibility;

- develop tolerance and understanding of others and begin to see the power of diversity in approaches to learning.

By the end of the course they will:

- have considered the characteristics, preferences and strengths of the four characters from the programme, which will help them find their way and stay on course for the journey of learning and life that lies ahead;

- have considered their own characteristics, preferences and strengths, and where they fit into the bigger picture;

- see school work in a new light and begin to break down their own personal barriers to studentship;

- have started a new journey towards personal growth;

- have developed more positive attitudes to studying and experienced the beginning of a life-long friendship with study.

ReadyStudyGo! complements other forms of pastoral teaching by:

- presenting a particular view of personalised learning and providing the materials to apply this in class;

- creating a forum in which the principles of Assessment for Learning such as goal setting, peer negotiation and self-assessment can be applied;

- supporting the implementation of Every Child Matters, focusing on how to help pupils enjoy and achieve and make a positive contribution.

ReadyStudyGo! is based on extensive research into the teaching of study skills, and presents a reappraisal of our understanding of what study is in order to teach better.

The lesson notes and the photocopiable resources have been developed over a number of years with children. The lessons are structured around conversations that take place in the 'studio'. These sessions encourage pupils to explore their thinking about study and school work in order to increase their levels of personal engagement and the possibility of success. This is a relaxed and fascinating process during which children gain and share new perspectives on themselves, their peers, school and life. Most of all, because the course focuses on a broader definition of what study is and because the pupils explore this idea in some depth, they begin to develop the resources and the strength to take more responsibility for their learning as they grow older.

Using the course

The sixteen conversations may be used in a continuous sequence once or twice a week over a half-term or term, or as an occasional resource. Their flexibility will suit your circumstances and pupils. Individual conversations can be quite contained or used as a springboard for wider exploration. Their duration is up to you. They can be introduced at the start of a year to help pupils focus on their approach in class or, for example, after KS2 SATs when the pupils can begin to explore being a student in preparation for transition to secondary school. The course can be used to create self-help support groups in form periods or tutor time for pupils in the early years of secondary school, setting the foundations for a positive approach to KS3/4.

To use the worksheets effectively, you will need the background that precedes the conversations. The teacher's role is that of a 'guide on the side', not 'sage on the stage'. The Teacher's Guide reviews 'study' and the subsequent chapters explain the structure and design principles of the course. The lesson notes and photocopiable resources provide specific guidance on the delivery of each conversation.

By setting up the studio sessions and working through the conversations and activities, you will support your pupils in building for themselves a personal world of imaginative characters, scenarios and possibilities that will help them to reframe their attitude to study. They will gain a powerful personal resource for their journey through the secondary school curriculum, and will develop a sense of the power they have to study independently now and in the future.

Working with the inner-world view

Before looking into the magical mansions of pupils' minds, it is good to spend a little time looking into our own. Our magical mansions are haunted. Sometimes we cannot see the phantoms – assumptions and expectations – that have the power to boost or hinder progress in learning. These ghosts can limit beliefs and therefore limit behaviour. For example, we might fail to help a child over a study threshold or barrier, simply because we resort to assumptions and expectations of what the teacher–pupil relationship should be. We don't glimpse what the child is really asking for or, through no fault of our own, we find ourselves complying with expected models of behaviour which are geared to the curriculum rather than to the private world and needs of the child.

Limiting self-beliefs arise in inner dialogue – intrapersonal conversations with the self. They are diminished by taking the opportunity to identify, explore and discuss them, bringing them out into the light of day. This is the purpose of *ReadyStudyGo!* We can think of this invisible inner engine of outward behaviour in terms of Gilbert Ryle's famous phrase: 'ghost in the machine'.

The ghost of study – the ideal student

Some of the ghosts have been around for a long time. One was reported by John Boswell in his critique of a text on study (1738), and yet many of the authors of today's study skills books still fall into the trap of writing what have been called 'cook books'. These books assume their reader to be an ideal student who will follow all the steps in the recipe and achieve success. As Selmes (1986) writes: 'These models of organised efficiency serve to emphasise the difference between the individual pupil and the ideal. In consequence, the advice would be alienating to many pupils who already feel somewhat inadequate'. The ideal student is the student in your head – a student who is as you would expect a good student to be. The definition of 'good' is determined by your often unconscious mental model: the ghost in your machine.

Jenny Mosley, in designing her Quality Circle Time model, cited the phantom of the ideal student and noted how it influences our behaviour on behaviour: 'Don't forget, when we ask a child to "behave well", we are imposing on him our image of an ideal child and there may be too big a mismatch between this ideal self and his actual self for him to cope with' (Mosley 1996).

Inappropriate expectations can leave pupils demotivated and so we need first of all to notice what level of expectation we project on our pupils in terms of the ideal student – or, at least, we should recognise when our conversations and actions are being influenced by this ghost in our machine. Other ghosts in the machine may well begin to appear. In the course of this book they will be exorcised.

Other ghosts

Here are six more ghosts, ones that seem to have influenced the requirements made of teachers in the UK over recent years. They drive decisions that affect teachers and constrain what can be done in classrooms to help pupils discover a love of study:

- 'School is about delivering content' (it's what I have termed 'postal').

- 'The teacher needs to talk' (tell, not gell).

- 'Education is all about results' (evidence, legality, accountability).

- 'Pupils have to meet targets all the time and arrive at certain points of accomplishment to order' (arrival, not journey).

- 'The arrival point on any particular learning journey is more likely to be forty minutes away than forty years' (short-term thinking).

- 'The pastoral dimension is of less importance than the academic in relation to performance' (not important as it is not examined).

And what about pupils? The ghosts of 'I can't' and 'I'm not good enough' are all too apparent.

A PERSONAL JOURNEY

In designing a study skills course for younger pupils, I initially prepared and delivered lessons that involved the usual study skills: memory, layout, highlighting, exam techniques, summarising, and so on. I found that repeated emphasis on mechanical skills brought little evidence of progress or transference to other learning contexts, and I realised that I had fallen into the trap of creating another subject.

I came to understand that there was an unexplored link between pastoral teaching and the teaching of study skills. Just as pupils have relationships with each other that affect their learning, so children have a relationship to study which affects their learning.

An unresolved relationship with study can create barriers to progress in school, inhibiting the development of independent learning characteristics and, for some children, creating a block to study. I wanted my pupils to be best friends with study rather than worst friends.

The emphasis in this book is therefore on studentship rather than study skills. The focus is on qualities of approach. Skill development was more successful and transferable once a strong qualitative foundation had been laid. We had interesting conversations in which we explored and attempted to answer some important questions:

- What is study?

- Who am I 'being' as a student?

- Why should I study?

- What's in it for me?

- How do I think?

- How do I study best?

- How do others study best?

TEACHER'S GUIDE

Understanding study

There are hundreds of study skills books available on the shelves. But most of them put the skills before the qualities of studentship. In previous centuries, we used the word 'study' differently. William Fulbeck (1600) outlined the 'qualities and sufficiencies . . . wherewith the student . . . ought to be furnished'. They were humility, a willingness to confess ignorance, temperance, diligence, a fired-up resolution to succeed, and 'courtesie' or mildness.

The emphasis was on qualities rather than skills, at least up to the 1900s. Conversely, the majority of the study skills texts today are not really about study skills at all, but about examination skills. They are driven to present mechanical skills. The historical view of study is a much more powerful motivator for children and their teachers than our narrow modern view of study. Taking the wider view, study can be described as a commitment to personal development and growth. It gives purpose and direction, and it motivates.

I meet many dispirited teachers and pupils while doing INSET. Many are aching for something more meaningful and worthwhile. The requirement to deliver the curriculum and meet targets reduces teachers' opportunities to engage in meaningful conversation. Teacher–pupil relationships break down when locked within a system that discourages personal interaction.

The emphasis on skills for study has arisen from the dominant role of measurement in our school system. This has led to underemphasis on the personal dimensions and dynamics of learning. The emphasis is on the system. It is not a view that all teachers support, yet all teachers find themselves focusing on the mechanical delivery of the curriculum and on devising better ways of delivering content so that it can be learned and mastered. This means that teaching becomes a 'postal' affair, concerned with receiving knowledge, and paying little attention to how students 'live' mentally and approach their task from an inner world view. Study is a very personal affair, a simple truth we have forgotten as a principle for guiding classroom practice.

We need to discover how individual pupils characterise study and school, and to pay as much attention to the personal dimensions of studentship as to the material and bureaucratic dimensions of the curriculum. A reassessment of study helps teachers and pupils work together and create dynamic and engaged relationships. Making 'I' contact is the gift of the memorable teacher and the joy of the memorable student.

Lessons from the research

The research into study skills carried out in the late 1970s and early 1980s (Tabberer 1987, for example) tended to lose momentum with the impact of the National Curriculum. In higher education research has continued to be funded. Early work includes that of Entwistle (1979), who established the ASI (Approaches to Study Inventory) in 1981; and progresses through Gibbs (1994) to the present day. Entwistle is currently working on a fourth revision of the ASI – the ALSI. The Improving Student Learning symposia have created an international platform for research into higher education studentship for thirteen years. There is much in the higher education research that is of interest to teachers in schools and relevant to this course.

Baxter-Magolda (2002) expresses studentship in terms of self-authorship:

- the capacity to define internally one's beliefs, identity, and relations with the world;

- a coherent sense of self.

ReadyStudyGo! (*RSG!*) provides opportunities for teachers and younger students to explore the aspects of belief, identity, relations and self that are central to developing a 'deep' approach to study. It is based on an affective understanding of study which emphasises self, rather than an effective one which emphasises results and outcomes. The affective dimension is explained in more detail later.

The research highlighted other 'qualities and sufficiencies'.

Emphasis on self-improvement

Self-improvement was a big thing in late nineteenth-century Britain. The university extension movement provided the opportunity for working people to extend their learning through attending summer schools. *RSG!* seeks to recover and encourage this historical understanding of study as a route to self-improvement – to becoming a better, more tolerant, understanding and self-aware student. The adult personal development agenda, so popular in books, magazines and on TV, also belongs in schools and colleges. Planning our teaching around pupil self-improvement helps pupils to make 'I' contact and break down the barriers to study from the inside out.

Deep students are good teachers

Research carried out in the late 1970s at Gothenburg (Marton and Säljö, reported in Entwistle and Ramsden 1983), shows that there are times when pupils adopt a surface approach (usually least successful) and times when they adopt a deep approach (usually much more successful). The approach an individual student takes in different circumstances is critical. The approach depends on how a student personally perceives and processes the learning context, environment and teaching style. The characteristics and qualities of the student who takes a deep approach are best summarised by stating that 'deep' students are their own best teacher.

RSG! aims to make this quality of self-teaching explicit and accessible for other students. Helping them practise self-teaching will move them from surface to deep approaches to study. Self-evaluation and reflection are therefore key elements in the course.

Making meaning is at the heart of learning

One world view of education sees school as a place in which the concrete and discrete objects of curriculum content built up by experts over centuries are transmitted into the brains of the receiving pupils. If the pupils pick up the transmission and can prove they have done so by transmitting the information back to the source, all is well. If they cannot do that, then they are in some way deficient. This world view can be described as objectivist.

The alternative world view is that the objectivist model is only good for some contexts and is incapable of describing the whole nature of education. What makes learning powerful is the extent to which it occurs inside the mind of the student. The more we know about how a pupil thinks about what they are learning and the meaning they are making of what they are learning in their head, the more powerful we can be as teachers. We need to keep learning as well as teaching. Pupils need to teach as well as learn. This world view is known as constructivist.

RSG! takes the constructivist view. Let us develop our pupils' thinking about study.

When study is taught through a personal and conversational approach using a constructivist model, the development of pupils' self-power in approaching study is better supported. Focusing on the personal approach to study provides a pastoral pathway to academic progress because it opens up an enquiry into what it is to be human and alive.

A mind once stretched by a new idea never returns to its original dimension.
Oliver Wendell-Holmes Jr

COURSE STRUCTURE

The short story 'The Amazing Tale of the Mysterious Magical Mansion' involves four characters. The sixteen conversations that follow are based on the story and provide opportunities for pupils to explore their world and the meaning of the characters. It provides characterisations for pupils to compare themselves to and reflect on.

The Magical Mansion

If a teacher is indeed wise, he does not bid you enter the house of his wisdom, but rather leads you to the threshold of your own mind.
Kahlil Gibran 1926

The Magical Mansion provides a location in which to anchor visualisations and to introduce and contextualise the characters. The children visualise and discuss the characters in the story and their setting in the Magical Mansion in some detail. The mansion is a metaphor for what we might think of as the ancestral seat of learning – the inner mind – of each child. It is a visual mnemonic, an emblem which will help the children understand study. Yates (1966) explains that emblematic visualisation is a technique that we have employed for centuries.

Overall, the Magical Mansion is:

> a holding environment that provides both welcoming acknowledgement to exactly who the person is right now as he or she is, and fosters the person's psychological evolution. As such, a holding environment is a tricky, transitional culture, an evolutionary bridge, a context for crossing over (Kegan 1994) . . .

Creating the Magical Mansion Gang

Bloom (1956) has influenced educational thought and policy for fifty years. He explored thinking as the cognitive domain. However, in 1964, Krathwohl, Bloom and Masia published a work that is often overlooked today. It explored the power and influence of movement in learning (the psycho-motor domain) and of feeling (the affective domain). These distinctions between thinking, movement and feeling provide the three H's – Head, Hand and Heart – which form the basis for the development of the characters in the Magical Mansion Gang.

1   Head: the cognitive domain – thinking

This domain includes remembering and reproducing what has been learnt, reordering material, and combining it with ideas, methods and procedures. In terms of study, this is about thinking and making meaning. A study skills curriculum wanting to develop a 'head' approach (to get your head round it) might include such topics as:

- memory techniques;
- information handling;
- preparing for testing and examinations;
- note taking and making;
- essay writing;
- revision techniques.

We can identify two characteristic approaches to study within the 'head' domain. We know that different learners approach learning tasks in different ways and, similarly, characterise information and create understanding in different ways. Research has focused on these differences since the 1950s (Bruner, Goodnow and Austin 1956). Pask's work in the late 1970s established the difference between 'serialist' and 'holist' approaches to learning (Pask 1975, 1976). Riding and Raynor (1998) point out that this is a continuing distinction in the research up to the 1990s, and map out 'analytical' and 'holistic' approaches that arise in the learning-styles literature. There is at present debate about how these styles of approach to learning can be identified and described – and even if they have any scientific validity (see Coffield *et al.* 2004) – but we could argue that this is an analytical view that may be overlooking some of the holistic advantages of identifying approaches to cognition in learning.

In order to capture the idea that different approaches are possible, the 'head' domain is represented in 'The Amazing Tale of the Mysterious Magical Mansion' by the twins Katy Kite, who represents the student who takes a more holist or global approach, and Pixel Pete, who represents the analytical student who takes a 'local' approach.

The two types have been described (Grabowski and Jonassen 1993) as follows:

Holists use a global, thematic approach to learning by concentrating first on building broad descriptions. The holistic learner typically focuses on several aspects of the subject at the same time and has many goals and working topics that span various levels . . . The holist then uses complex links to relate multi-level information. Higher ordered relationships are established, essentially using a top-down approach . . . Interconnections between theoretical, practical, and personal aspects of a topic are made through the use of analogies, illustrations, and anecdotes.

Serialists use an 'operations' approach to learning, concentrating more narrowly on details and procedures before conceptualizing an overall picture. They typically combine information in a linear sequence, focusing on small chunks of information that are low in the hierarchical structure, and working from the bottom up. The serialists work step-by-step within this narrow framework, concentrating on well-defined and sequentially ordered chunks that can be related using simple links.

It is hoped that pupils using the *RSG!* course will become aware of their strengths with regard to these types. Having explored these possibilities, they have the opportunity to begin the journey towards becoming what Pask called versatile learners. Those students employ holist and serialist learning strategies. They are able to use global and detailed, local approaches. Versatile students are proficient at most types of study.

Pask also identified learning pathologies – deficiencies arising from a strong basis in a single style. The holist learner's deficiency is overdependence on analogies and metaphor. Pask called this 'globetrotting'. The serialist learner's deficiency is an inability to make connections at a conceptual level, which he called 'improvidence'. These deficiencies point out the value of allowing children to explore and develop wider approaches to learning through the studio conversations.

2 Hand: the psycho-motor domain – action/doing

This domain is about organising objects and physical things. A study skills curriculum that wants to develop the 'hand' approach might include such topics as:

- organisation of materials;

- access to sources;

- physical learning methods.

This domain is represented in the story by the characterisation of Handy Sam.

3 Heart: the affective domain – feeling

This domain comprises 'objectives which emphasise a feeling tone, an emotion, or a degree of acceptance or rejection' (Krathwohl, Bloom and Masia 1964). In terms of study, this relates to attitude, readiness and approach. A study skills curriculum wanting to develop the 'heart' approach might include such topics as:

- affection;

- inspiration;

- excitement;

- engagement;

- self-awareness;

- understanding of others;

- commitment to longer-term goals;

- love of learning.

The affective domain is at the heart of *RSG!* We can think of this domain as the best place to be in order to conduct conversations to develop qualities of studentship and create positive approaches to study. Focusing on this domain in particular will help us to create personal engagement and maintain the 'I' contact with pupils. In past times, we used to acknowledge that we study something for the love of it. The *Shorter Oxford English Dictionary* (2002) reports one of the seventeenth-century definitions of the word 'study' as 'affection'. Affection engages us and moves us to be students.

This domain of studentship is represented in the story by Felix Hart.

The following table (Photocopiable 0.1, pages 14–15) summarises the key characteristics of the four, enabling direct comparison of their qualities. In Conversations 1 and 9 there are outlines of the characters (Photocopiable 1.4, page 36; Photocopiable 9.3, page 78).

Key Characteristics Page 1

➤ The following table summarises key characteristics of the Magical Mansion Gang. Use the blank spaces to add some more characteristics.

Pixel Pete	Katy Kite	Handy Sam	Felix Hart
Thinking – Analysis	Thinking – Conceptual	Doing	Feeling
Major characteristics			
left-brain	right-brain	outward physical	inward feeling
quantity	quality	quantity	quality
effective	affective	effective	affective
objective	subjective	objective	subjective
knowledge	reflection and insight	action	empathy
instrumentation	wonder	tools	conversation
Other characteristics			
analytical	creative	active	6 basic emotions:
neat	arty	manual	1 happy
orderly	synthesis	energy	2 sad
judges	quiet	muscular	3 angry
categorises	intuitive	manager	4 scared
separates out	inventive	gets things done	5 excited
logical	philosopher	performs	6 tender
intellectual	poet	vigour	vulnerable
time focused	self-aware	carries out orders	moody
arranged	insightful	sorted	understanding
often in charge	sees implications	organised	expressive
right and wrong	past and future	pulls together	subjective
black and white	powerful	gets to grips	confident
literal	perceptive	good time management	needs/gives approval
needs evidence	possibilities	practical	needs/gives smiles
	conceptual	down to earth	needs to feel safe
	head in the clouds	strong handshake	caring
			motivator
			respectful
			gentle/sensitive

0.1

Key Characteristics Page 2

➤ The following table summarises more key characteristics of the Magical Mansion Gang. Use the blank spaces to add some more characteristics.

Pixel Pete	Katy Kite	Handy Sam	Felix Hart
Thinking – Analysis	Thinking – Conceptual	Doing	Feeling
Strengths			
worksheets	creativity	hands on	group discussion
manuals	deep thought	practical	listening
software	inspiration	materials	counselling
analysing	insight	hardware	empathy
calibration	new ideas	doing	understanding
measurement	solutions to problems	co-ordination	sympathy
books	books		encouragement
research	reflection		beliefs/values
planning	working individually		ethics
	meditation		courage
			rising to the challenge
			motivation
			in touch with feelings
			explaining feelings
			appreciation
			humour
Fears			
making mistakes	real world	thinking too long	disapproval
change	losing freedom to contemplate	sitting too long	rejection
unknowns	lists and tables	listening too long	failure to live up to expectations
loss of security	planning		being bullied
loss of possessions	analysis		conflict
missing the inference	measures		loneliness
being unprepared			non-caring others
co-operating in groups			dogmatism

CREATING AN AFFECTIVE APPROACH

This section explains the various elements of this affective course. *RSG!* is designed as a journey. It is process-based, and focused firmly on the development of potential. It teaches through conversation and promotes personal growth.

1 Journey

. . . to be educated is not to arrive at a destination but to travel with a different point of view.
R.S. Peters 1963

We use the word 'course' to describe a process of lessons. We talk of our wish to 'motivate' pupils – to keep them moving towards their learning goals. We ask 'Where did we get to yesterday?' We plan a scheme of guided steps to help pupils explore different angles and reach certain stages and levels of achievement. These ways of talking about teaching and learning show how deeply rooted the locational metaphor of the learning journey is. When children stop moving or see that they can no longer make progress, they become demotivated and stop or get stuck. We want them to be motivated about study, so *RSG!* is designed as a journey.

2 Process

Knowing is a process, not a product.
Jerome Bruner 1966

The 'outward' conversations and activities of *RSG!* create an 'inward' journey. This process is the key to movement and so, the identification of a body of content to be delivered for learning and for students to reproduce under specific circumstances has been avoided. The identification of a series of discrete skills to be acquired and practised has also been avoided. Taking one or both of these approaches would simply have tipped the course back into the mechanical postal mode.

Instead, the course is a carefully structured yet subjective exploration of ideas and insights, involving sharing thinking and uncovering limiting assumptions and attitudes. It includes discussion, reflection, discovery and self-evaluation. This process-based approach recognises the power of personal involvement in the creation of deeper studentship. In making the journey together, teachers learn from pupils and pupils learn both from their peers and from within their own untapped resources. The guided conversations prompt pupils to recognise what they think about study, and to begin to understand how this determines their approach to school and supports them in making adjustments over time. It sets up opportunities for higher-order thinking in terms of analysis, synthesis and evaluation.

In taking this approach, teachers can attend to the mental and attitudinal growth of their pupils – which, for many, lies at the heart of their love of teaching.

3 Development – an unfolding

The word 'develop' comes from the old French word *desveloper*, which means to 'unfold, uncover, reveal, bring to light'. *The Shorter Oxford English Dictionary* also lists: 'Unfold more fully: bring out all that is potentially contained in; bring out from latent to an active or visible state; make fuller . . .; cause to grow or mature, evolve (from, out of); cause to come into existence.'

Development is, therefore, a process of unfolding over time. I like to think of *RSG!* as a journey of unfolding. Many teachers have experienced the child in their class who started the year with low self-esteem but who, through patient and attentive nurturing, has unfolded into a stronger, more confident and self-assured young person. If you would like to explore this idea further, see *Dibbs: In Search of Self* by Virginia Axline (1964).

RSG! will help pupils to unfold within themselves as students and develop a more positive inner 'study voice'. This will help them to break down the barriers to study from the inside out.

4 Potential

The commoness of self-power thus awakened was . . . of immense value and, animated by it, the progress of the class was astonishing.
John Macaulay, quoted in Tyndall 1897

Potential relates to untapped power. Paradoxically, taking the process-based approach provides the means of unlocking potential and helping pupils perform better at the mechanical skills of study in due course. Once their self-power is ignited, it is much more likely that they will teach themselves how best to find out more and learn, just as pupils do with complex computer programs and games. They will develop the skills not through being required to learn them, but through the awakening of self-power in pursuit of personally relevant goals.

We all have self-power. Sometimes it is locked away and we have forgotten where the key is – or that there is a key. If only we could unlock the door to the study where the power lives in the magical mansion of their minds. *RSG!* is focused on unlocking potential, on helping pupils find their own key. It is a counter-balance to the product/outcomes-based curriculum activities that may dominate our interactions with pupils in classrooms.

5   Conversation

RSG! sets up the opportunities for conversation with the Magical Mansion Gang. Conversation engages us. Talk is effective, but conversation is affective. It taps into the affective domain and helps to create the personal involvement of pupils through 'I' contact.

Conversation is a meeting of minds with different memories and habits. When minds meet, they don't just exchange facts: they transform them, reshape them, draw different implications from them, engage in new trains of thought. Conversation doesn't just shuffle the cards: it creates new cards . . . In the process one can change one's idea of beauty, and when that happens, one is changed oneself.
T. Zeldin 1998

Positive transformations of mind, the development of self-power and the creation of new trains of thought are all affective issues. One of the most direct routes to that domain is through the setting up of conversations for engagement in the classroom.

Decades of research have shown, moreover, that study can be more successful when conducted in interpersonal social settings. However, by tapping into the power of conversation, *RSG!* goes further by paying particular attention to the intrapersonal dimensions of study – that is, how pupils talk to themselves about study.

Pask (1975) developed a 'conversational theory of learning' on the basis of finding that students worked towards a full understanding of a subject by questioning and trying out ideas, either on a teacher or an *alter ego* which he considered to be 'another part of the mind which monitored and interacted with the learning process'. This seems to allude to the idea of a learning self. Creating engaging conversations that reveal both external and internal dialogue with the learning self is a central feature of the *RSG!* approach. It is achieved through a relationship with the characters in the Magical Mansion Gang based on the three H's (see pages 11–13).

6   Growth

Plato is said to have taught in a planted suburb of Athens from the name for which we derive the word 'academy'. The garden is a metaphor for growth. Academies promote personal growth, and academia is concerned with the growth of the mind. We can reinterpret the idea of academic curricula to include personal engagement which, in addition to the growth of knowledge, leads to personal growth and an increase in the capacity to be a versatile student.

TEACHING APPROACH

The quality of your approach as facilitator will determine the quality of the sessions and the quality of the learning. So what is the best way to approach the *RSG!* process?

The ghost busters

We have already identified the 'ghosts in the machine' (see pages 7–8). Here are some ghost-busting ideas about study. These determine the approach of the teacher in facilitating conversations in studio time:

- Study succeeds when it is understood as a personal and not just a postal affair. Get in touch with what the pupil thinks about study. Make eye contact – make 'I' contact.

- Study is more about safe and shared conversation than about teacher talk.

- Study succeeds at least as much on the basis of aiming for affective (pastoral) development (the inward journey) as it does on effective (examination) outcomes (the outward arrival).

- Study success fundamentally requires qualities of approach working hand in hand with mechanical skills. Mechanical skills without the quality dimension do not take root.

- Successful students are taught both by teachers and by themselves. They somehow realise that they are on a journey of self-development – it's for them personally, not their teachers or their parents, and every investment of time and effort on their part adds to their personal stock. Self-teaching arises from an acknowledgement of personal responsibility.

- Study success comes from setting longer-term goals 'in mind', which can give a deep sense of purpose. Where are you growing?

Creating a thinking environment™

In *Time to Think*, Nancy Kline (1999) teaches about 'listening to ignite the human mind'. In her approach, listening without judgement is the key to helping someone learn to think for themselves. It is possible to 'hold' someone in your listening, and by not interrupting you immediately set off a whole series of subtle events that allow the person to think more deeply. Here are some of Kline's guidelines for setting up a thinking environment:

- Everything we do depends for its quality on the thinking we do first. Our thinking depends on the quality of our attention for each other.

- Thinking at its best is not just a cool act of cerebration. It is also a thing of the heart.

- A 'thinking environment' is the set of ten conditions under which human beings can think for themselves – with rigour, imagination, courage and grace.

- Listening of this calibre ignites the human mind.

Here are the ten components of the thinking environment:

1 *Attention* Listening with respect, interest and fascination

2 *Incisive questions* Removing assumptions that limit ideas

3 *Equality* Treating each other as thinking peers
     i   Giving equal turns and attention
     ii   Keeping agreements and boundaries

4 *Appreciation* Practising a five-to-one ratio of appreciation to criticism

5 *Ease* Offering freedom from rush or urgency

6 *Encouragement* Moving beyond competition

7 *Feelings* Allowing sufficient emotional release to restore thinking

8 *Information* Providing a full and accurate picture of reality

9 *Place* Creating a physical environment that says to people 'You matter'

10 *Diversity* Adding quality because of the differences between us.

This is an excellent set of guidelines for *RSG!* conversations. The following list offers advice in a different form.

- **Listen:** You can help someone else think by listening without interruption. They will thank you for letting them think.

- **Praise:** Use praise to help someone think better. Reward them with friendly and encouraging questions and answers. Smile. Give them eye contact while they think and talk.

- **Respect:** Treat everyone as you would like to be treated yourself. Show respect for their ideas, thinking and talking.

- **Relax:** Help make the atmosphere in the studio a good one. We can all do our best thinking when there is no threat or worry.

- **Express:** Feel free to say what you are really thinking. You will not be judged by the others. This is because you have shown you are not going to judge anyone yourself.

- **Accept:** Always look out for how differences are, in fact, strengths and not weaknesses. Hunt for strengths in what others say and do.

Unconditional positive regard

In the spirit of affective learning, *RSG!* helps you to steer the pupils towards conversations that will help you to 'draw out' (the meaning of the Latin word *educare/educere*) their thinking about study. Your stance in the *RSG!* conversations is best described using Carl Rogers' famous term: 'unconditional positive regard'. As the *RSG!* conversations support your children in making their personal views of study visible and available for public exploration, it is your role to encourage them to continue to express and share without judgement what they think, feel and do in terms of study. It is through positive conversations, in which children feel safe to reveal their innermost views on study, that *RSG!* will help you and your pupils to redefine their relationship to study.

Some of the pupils' private thoughts on study will be negative and sometimes very negative. Your ghost of 'how pupils should relate to teachers' may appear and you may find yourself saying that negative talk is not expected. However, in order to approach the affective development of their thinking, your role is to accept their thinking just where it is. Then they can externalise it and study it. This holding of negative thinking is a powerful signal, giving pupils permission to give you more thinking to explore. The more they can express and externalise the negative thinking, the less it will hold them to repeating old behaviour patterns based on a narrow view of possibilities.

Unconditional positive regard is the best way to progress both positive and negative thinking. Pupils may gain a sense of freedom from needing to perform against the examined curriculum and should, with your support, feel increasingly safe to express what they really think in genuine conversations. There are no right or wrong answers in this approach; instead there are interesting expressions of what they think. The *RSG!* materials will help pupils to explore their attitudes and assumptions in an imaginative way and to think both about themselves and others without making judgements or being judged.

When we help children to attend to qualities of thought in this way, and to understand themselves and their peers better as students, they become more motivated to develop their approach to study – not because they have to, but through the excitement of exploring new worlds of meaning and experience that open up to them in a magical way within their own minds.

Practical issues

Setting up the studio

The studio is a place to think, share and reflect on what study is and what being a student means. The classroom becomes a space where guided conversations take place that help pupils discover and model attitudes and behaviours that can then be bridged back into everyday life at school. These include eagerness, enthusiasm, spirit and pursuit. You can experiment with different groupings of tables, lighting, music, and so on, at appropriate points to signify that the studio is in session. Use the catch phrase 'Ready? Study? Go!' to signal the beginning of a session which might involve rearranging the room. The studio should allow the pupils both to work in a circle facing each other and to work at tables individually and in small groups.

Using music in the studio

Using music is a fantastic way to create atmosphere, to provide aural mnemonics for the pupils, and to introduce each of the four characters. Choose a piece of music that you feel represents each character and use it to support the work on that character. Some guidelines follow:

Pixel Pete

The use of music by Johann Sebastian Bach would fit with the logical approach of Pixel Pete. You could choose excerpts from Bach's piano fugues.

Katy Kite

The use of impressionist music would suit Katy Kite's contemplative nature. You could use 'Clair de Lune' from the *Suite Bergamasque* or 'La Cathédrale engloutie' from *Préludes* by Claude Debussy. You might also try 'On Hearing the First Cuckoo in Spring' from *Two Pieces for Light Orchestra* by Frederick Delius.

Felix Hart

Sweeping orchestral music can be used to signify the emotional ups and downs that Felix experiences. You could use the 'Fantasy Overture' from *Romeo and Juliet* by Tchaikovsky or excerpts from Rachmaninov's piano concertos.

Handy Sam

Theme music from an action movie may be appropriate to convey the practical nature of Handy Sam, but try to avoid excerpts from films named after the protagonist, such as *Superman* and *Spiderman*.

Once your pupils are sufficiently familiar with each character, you could ask them to make suggestions for pieces of music that they think represent each of them. They could compose and play their own musical motifs for the characters, choosing musical styles and instruments as appropriate. These could be combined into a single composition to represent the power of the characters working together. The performance of such compositions could be part of the acclamation and celebration at the end of the course.

A flexible process

As this is a process curriculum, the conversations can be introduced in the way that best suits your children and the time available. The number of times you call 'Ready? Study? Go!' each week, and the duration of each session, is your choice and will depend on the year group, the time of year and what is possible on the timetable. You may wish to call 'Ready? Study? Go!' because a situation arises concerning homework or revision or working in class which it will require thinking time in the studio to explore and resolve. The pupils may call the catchphrase in those circumstances.

Wandering off through personal stories and other anecdotal evidence is positively encouraged in order to allow the children to explore, explain and develop their underlying mental models of study. Some studio sessions may be longer than normal because everyone makes the most of a particularly exciting or deep conversation, or takes extra time to finish off drawing or written work.

Assessment

The course materials require the completion of writing and drawing tasks, but there is no testing. The emphasis instead is on formative assessment in terms of both self-and peer-evaluation. It is possible to link the *RSG!* conversations with your school's approach to Assessment for Learning. To assist in this, a series of self-evaluation questions is included in Conversation 1, on 'My *RSG!* Learning Log' (Photocopiable 1.5, page 37). This log can be used at the completion of each studio session or as otherwise required.

The pupil photocopy masters

These provide prompts and recording sheets for before, during and after studio conversations. They prompt drawing, annotation, some writing and plenty of discussion and the sharing of ideas. The children can be encouraged to put their own personal stamp and identity on them. By completing them, pupils produce a treasure-trove of insights into their own thinking about study and school work, and build up a record of their personal reflections on both themselves and others as students. They often take their worksheets home and share their thinking. The completed worksheets also provide an alternative profile to take to a new class or secondary school and prompt a meaningful and personal conversation with a new form tutor.

Trusting the process

Einstein said that we often value what is measurable rather than measure what is valuable. And yet, we can also say that some of the best and most valuable learning is intangible and not measurable – it is part of a process in which no evidence necessarily appears, and often outcomes are in the long term rather than the short term anyway.

It can feel a little risky to be open to the pupils' thinking and responses. It may take them a little while to understand that you are offering them the opportunity, and giving them the permission, to think for themselves and explore their views and attitudes about study with frankness, openness and integrity. Pupils may even resist thinking in this way as they are conditioned to being passive receptors of knowledge. But it is worthwhile to persevere and to teach them (by handing over the teaching) that they are the authors of their own thoughts and therefore of their lives. You may experience a dip in motivation initially as the more creative and open approach takes time to settle. Allow that time. Invite and celebrate their thinking. Take an interest in their personal views. Help pupils to observe and enjoy the silence that comes over someone as they think. Help them to give others the gift of thinking time.

We know that a deeper and wider meaning of study is about enrichment of their personal approach to school and life-long learning – for themselves, by themselves, with themselves, and with their friends. Let us help them to be ready for study – and to go.

BIBLIOGRAPHY

Axline, V. (1964) *Dibs: In Search of Self.* London: Penguin

Baxter-Magolda, M. (2002) *Learners' Narratives: Real-life Stories about Constructivist–Developmental Pedagogy.* Presentation at 10th Improving Student Learning Symposium: 'Improving Student Learning: Theory and Practice – 10 years on'

Bloom, B.S. (1956) *Taxonomy of Educational Objectives, Handbook I: The Cognitive Domain.* New York: David McKay Co. Inc.

Boswell, J. (1738) *A Method of Study.* London

Bruner, J. (1966) *Towards a Theory of Instruction.* Cambridge MA: Belkapp Press

Bruner, J., J.J. Goodnow and G.A. Austin (1956) 'The Process of Concept Attainment', in *A Study of Thinking.* New York: John Wiley & Sons

Caviglioli, O. and I. Harris (2004) *Reaching out to all Thinkers.* London: Network Continuum Education

Coffield, F. *et al.* (2004) *Learning Styles and Pedagogy in Post-16 Learning.* Learning and Skills Research Centre. Trowbridge: Cromwell Press

Dennison, P. and G. (1992) *Brain Gym: Simple Activities for Whole Brain Learning.* Ventura CA: Edu-Kinesthetics, Inc.

Dennison, P. and G. (1994) *Brain Gym: Teacher's Edition Revised.* Ventura CA: Edu-Kinesthetics, Inc.

Entwistle, N. (1979) *Motivation, Styles of Learning and the Academic Environment.* Edinburgh: University of Edinburgh (ERIC Document Reproduction Service No. ED 190 636)

Entwistle, N. and P. Ramsden (1983) *Understanding Student Learning.* London: Croom Helm

Fulbeck, W. (1600) *A Direction or Preparative to the Study of the Lawe.* London

Gibbs, G. (ed.) (1994) *Improving Student Learning. Theory and Practice.* Oxford: The Oxford Centre for Staff Development

Gibran, K. (1926) *The Prophet.* London: William Heinemann

Goldblum, N. (2001) *The Brain Shaped Mind.* Cambridge: Cambridge University Press

Grabowski, B.L. and D.H. Jonassen (1993) *Handbook of Individual Differences, Learning and Instruction.* Mahwah NJ: Lawrence Erlbaum Associates

Harvey, E.R. (1976) *The Inward Wits: Psychological Theory in the Middle Ages and the Renaissance,* ed. E.H. Gombrich and J.P. Trapp. London: Warburg Institute Surveys

Hoffman, E. (1999) *The Learning Adventure.* London: Learn to Learn

Hubbard, L.R. (2000) *Learning to Learn.* St Louis MO: Effective Education Publishing

Kegan, R. (1994) *In Over our Heads.* Cambridge MA: Harvard University Press

Kline, N. (1999) *Time to Think. Listening to Ignite the Human Mind.* London: Ward Lock

Krathwohl, D.R., B.S. Bloom and B.B. Masia (1964) *Taxonomy of Educational Objectives, Book 2: Affective Domain.* New York: Longman

Marton, F. and R. Säljö (1997) 'Approaches to Learning' in F. Marton, D. Hounsell and N. Entwistle (eds.) *The Experience of Learning.* Edinburgh: Scottish Academic Press

Mosley, J. (1996) *Quality Circle Time in the Primary Classroom.* Cambridge: LDA

Paredes, J.A. and M.J. Hepburn (1976) 'The Split-brain and the Culture-cognition Paradox'. *Current Anthropology,* 17

Parkin, M. (1998) 'Giant Steps' in M. Parkin (ed.) *Tales for Trainers.* London: Kogan Page

Pask, G. (1975) *Conversation, Cognition and Learning.* Amsterdam: Elsevier

Pask, G. (1976) 'Styles and Strategies of Learning'. *British Journal of Educational Psychology,* 46, 128-148

Peters, R.S. (1963) *Education as Initiation.* Presented as part of inaugural lecture at the London Institute of Education

Riding, R. and S.G. Rayner (1998) *Cognitive Styles and Learning Strategies.* London: David Fulton

Rogers, C.R. (1951) *Client-centered Therapy: Its Current Practice, Implications and Theory.* Boston: Houghton Mifflin

Selmes, I.P. (1986) 'Approaches to Normal Learning Tasks adopted by Senior Secondary School Pupils'. *British Educational Research Journal,* 12, 15

Shorter Oxford English Dictionary (2002) Fifth edition, Oxford: Oxford University Press

Sternberg, R.J. and W.M. Williams (1998) *Intelligence, Instruction, and Assessment: Theory into Practice.* Hillsborough NJ: Lawrence Erlbaum Associates

Sternberg, R.J. and L. Zhang, (2001) *Perspectives on Thinking, Learning, and Cognitive Styles.* Mahwah NJ: Lawrence Erlbaum Associates

Tabberer, R. (1987) *Study and Information Skills in Schools.* British Library R & R Report 5870. London: Delmar Publishing

Tyndall, J. (1897) *Fragments of Science: A Series of Detached Essays and Reviews.* New York: D. Appleton & Co.

Vygotsky, L.S. (1978) *Mind and Society: The Development of Higher Mental Processes.* Cambridge MA: Harvard University Press

Yates, F. (1966) The Art of Memory. Chicago: University of Chicago Press

Zeldin, T. (1998) *Conversation.* London: Harvill Press

Web references

The Oxford Centre for Staff and Learning Development: www.brookes.ac.uk/services/ocsd

Classical language sources and definitions: www.perseus.tufts.edu

LESSON NOTES FOR STUDIO CONVERSATIONS

Process

The notes for each conversation that follow are designed to generate personal exploration and reflection. Each conversation is a starting point in a process and not an end-point. The conversations are prompts that invite you to explore ideas freely and interact with your pupils in the way that you know best suits them.

Structure

Each set of notes is divided into three sections:

■ APPROACH

The background information to help you quickly get your head round the main thrust of the lesson and hit the ground running.

■ ACTION

The activities, tasks and questions. Often includes one or more games to embed the learning. A number of these games take place in a circle. The use of a circle for games and activities is an ancient tradition. Thanks to the work of Jenny Mosley and others, wider circle time models are established ways of working in many schools.

■ APPRAISAL

Ideas on how to follow up generally or to create a link to the next conversation, or both.

➤ The *RSG!* Round

Each conversation ends with an opportunity to play the 'I contact' game. This helps pupils reflect on their thoughts, feelings and actions on the topics and activities that have come up as part of the conversation in one or more studio sessions. Use 'The Three H's Capture Lists' 1 and 2 (Photocopiables 0.2 and 0.3, pages 26 and 27) to record the ideas and responses. For further explanation of the three H's see pages 11 to 13.

➤ The *RSG!* Round: Making 'I' contact

Resources 'The Three H's Capture Lists' (Photocopiables 0.2 and/or 0.3).

Aim To capture thinking, doing and feeling responses after a session or series of sessions and to create empathy and further discussion on issues raised.

What to do Pupils sit in a circle and take turns to answer the questions on the photocopiable(s). Go round the circle for each question.

After the session, the pupils may record their ideas and responses on 'The Three H's Capture Lists'.

The Three H's Capture List 1

> **Head**

Use this to record findings and ideas when addressing a particular issue or learning task.

How do you think about this?
Pixel Pete

How do you think about this?
Katy Kite

The Three H's Capture List 2

➤ **Hand and heart**

Use this to record findings and ideas when addressing a particular issue or learning task.

What might you do about this?
Handy Sam

How do you feel about this?
Felix Hart

THE AMAZING TALE OF THE MAGICAL MANSION

■ APPROACH

The story provides the organising ideas and characters on which the rest of the course is built. The characters in the story are based on the three H's and encourage the pupils to think imaginatively about the course materials from the start.

Goldblum (2001) points out that neuroscientific research underlines the importance of story in learning. The tradition of representing the world of the mind as an interior goes back through Freud to both ancient and medieval times (Harvey 1976). That the mind can, as an interior space, be bigger on the inside than the outside is an idea that has exercised philosophers for centuries and is one of the features of the Magical Mansion. I have found that pupils can make real strides in their thinking about study simply by using the mansion metaphor. Drawing is encouraged throughout as it helps the pupils to process the information at a visual/kinaesthetic, more embedded level.

The story is in two parts. The first part introduces the two characters Pixel Pete and Katy Kite. They represent the two approaches to cognition – local and global. The second part of the story, which is in Conversation 9, introduces the other two characters, Handy Sam and Felix Hart. They represent doing/action and feeling.

■ ACTION

➤ 1 Game: Pass the Smile

Resources None.

Aim To establish eye contact and create a positive atmosphere.

What to do Smile at a child on your left or right, who then passes the smile round the circle until everyone is smiling.

➤ 2 Game: Forest Daydream

Resources CD player and recording of tranquil music.

Aim To enhance imagination skills.

What to do The pupils sit or lie with their eyes closed while you play a piece of tranquil music. Ask them to imagine a scene in which they are walking through a forest. Then they leave the forest and start to walk across a wide field to see what is on a distant headland. When they get to the other side of the field, they see an amazing mansion. What is it like? You could discuss what they imagined before moving on to part 3.

➤ 3 Read the story

While you read the story (Photocopiable 1.1, pages 30–33), encourage the pupils to build up the imaginative world in their mind. Ask them to visualise the characters and the story in as much detail as possible – like a huge film in their heads with all the Technicolor detail in place. The more successfully they engage with this visualisation at this stage, the more successfully they will engage with the rest of the material in the course.

THE AMAZING TALE OF THE MAGICAL MANSION

- Draw the twins and write descriptions of them on a copy of the characters worksheet (Photocopiable 1.2, page 34). They can draw the mansion on the back. Try to avoid showing the children any of the book's illustrations at this stage.

- Complete a copy of the worksheet 'Your Room' (Photocopiable 1.3, page 35).

- Hand out 'The Magical Mansion Gang: The Twins' worksheet (Photocopiable 1.4, page 36) and discuss the characters. To support you in building a more detailed understanding of the different characteristics of the twins and to encourage discussion, see 'Key Characteristics' (Photocopiable 0.1, pages 14–15). This table may be used as a prompt for the pupils, as a discussion stimulus or as a resource to organise your ideas for teaching.

- Do not debrief the story at this stage. It will be examined in some detail later.

APPRAISAL

➤ The *RSG!* Round: Making 'I' contact

Resources A copy of 'The Three H's Capture List 1' (Photocopiable 0.2, page 26) per child.

Aim To capture thinking, doing and feeling responses after a session or series of sessions and to create empathy and further discussion on issues raised.

What to do The pupils sit in a circle and take turns to answer the questions on 'The Three H's Capture List 1'. After the session they may write their conclusions on a copy of the worksheet.

Encourage pupils after this and all other conversations to fill in 'My *RSG!* Learning Log' (Photocopiable 1.5, page 37)

Having read the story, the pupils are taken away from the Magical Mansion for a while in order to be introduced to some key ideas to support them for the rest of the journey and to allow the visualisations to settle. They begin to explore, next, the concepts of preferences and characteristics. Having become a little more expert in understanding and spotting preferences and characteristics in others and themselves, the pupils will later apply their thinking to the characters of the Magical Mansion Gang and identify their own strengths.

A focus on characteristics and preferences aims to increase self-awareness in terms of understanding study and, it is hoped, will encourage empathy, tolerance and understanding of other pupils. Seeing individual differences between pupils as strengths and not weaknesses is a key element of the course design.

The Amazing Tale of the
Mysterious Magical Mansion page 1

Once upon a time and not very far away, high up on top of a high, high headland, there was a magical mansion from where, it was said, you could see the whole world.

Passers-by said that, from the outside, the mansion looked like a normal-sized mansion: with east and west wings, lots of windows, a grand entrance hall and staircase, numerous rooms, and all around a beautiful garden. But people said that, if you ever got the chance of looking inside (few people ever took that chance), you would discover that the inside seemed bigger than the outside. It was even said by some that the Magical Mansion was so big inside that there was no limit to the size and number of rooms it could hold. You could put a whole galaxy or even a universe in there!

There was something else that the people had heard about the Magical Mansion. You could put as much furniture and other things as you liked into each of the rooms, and they would change to fit whatever you put in, leaving plenty of space to move around. The rooms never became crowded or cramped. Everything just fitted somehow.

Now, the locals often talked about the Magical Mansion. They wished they could live in a house like that, instead of their tiny little cottages and hovels which had no room to move around in and certainly no room for expansion. Thinking about the Magical Mansion made them feel quite small. The big question on everyone's lips was 'Who owns the Magical Mansion?' Although it was rumoured that four friends lived there, no one knew who they were and no one had ever heard the name of the owner.

We are going to find out all these things. We are going to go on a journey that will take us to the Magical Mansion, and we shall meet the characters who live there.

There are indeed four of them. These four friends minded the mansion for the owner.

Each of them had different views on everything. Two of them were twins. They were always noticing that they saw the world differently. These two, the twins, were called Katy Kite and Pixel Pete. They were what we sometimes call mirror twins. One was left-handed, the other right-handed.

The Amazing Tale of the
Mysterious Magical Mansion page 2

When they tried to achieve things on their own they were rather one-sided in their approach. They couldn't help it – it was who they were. In each of their ways, they were very, very talented. The good news is that they discovered (only very recently) a secret that helped them to join up their talents and become versatile thinkers.

The twins minded the mansion every day. Pixel Pete went round the rooms in order, following a system he had invented. Katy Kite moodled around. She wandered and puttered about. Both, in their own way, looked after the many, many rooms and discovered and rediscovered what was in them. They loved the old place. Many of the rooms had precious and wonderful things in them. Other rooms (way up beyond the creaky staircase in the dim and dark distance) were rather scary. Some of the rooms were quite new. The paint was still wet on the doors, and the door knobs gleamed. Other rooms were old and their doors were covered in cobwebs. Their door knobs were dimmed with lack of use and everything was covered with a thick layer of dust. They had the old, musty smell of rooms that had not been visited for a long time. There was even one room they had not been into – a mystery room right at the centre of the house.

Our twin minders had wandered into all the other rooms at some point. But there were so many rooms that each of them could not possibly look into every one every day. Some of the rooms had not been visited for a very long time. There were some rooms that Katy Kite and Pixel Pete didn't want to go back to unless they really had to. Others were visited almost every day.

The rooms quietly waited for the twins to come and visit. Behind their doors, they held their contents – waiting for the door to creak open one day, a chink of light to appear, and Katy Kite and Pixel Pete to peer round the door frame to see what had been placed in there. If only they looked inside, the lights would become magically brighter until everything was clear.

Because of the power of his two minders (although they often did not realise that they had this power) the owner of the Magical Mansion was himself rather special and had many gifts. He was very clever – more clever than any computer and certainly more clever than anything else in the known universe. It was amazing what the twins could do when they put their minds together and became versatile.

Yet, despite the talents of the twins, the owner wasn't always confident. In fact, he sometimes didn't realise how clever he was. Did you know that many pupils do not know how clever they are? They don't think it's possible to be clever and they never open the doors to their Magical Mansion.

The Amazing Tale of the Mysterious Magical Mansion page 3

Let's meet the twins.

Katy Kite liked to discover the big ideas behind things in life. She went for the big story. She liked themes. She liked day-dreaming, and she used her imagination a lot. She loved to fly her kite on windy days. As she did so, she imagined herself flying above everything, seeing patterns and meanings that others couldn't see. When she was dreaming, she would look outside the window or focus on the ceiling with a far-away look in her eyes.

Katy Kite loved music and dancing, and she was good at finding her way around. She did tend to get distracted sometimes and wander off with her kite, but she'd always find her way back! When she had been away, she always came back with some fascinating new object which she placed somewhere special in the Magical Mansion. She always had stories to tell.

Pixel Pete, on the other mind, was precise. He focused on the detail. He was logical and analytical about things. He liked to keep his feet on the ground and wanted clear answers to questions. He loved language and lists and reading and logic, of course! He was good at puzzles and maths and he always enjoyed those games where you have to put things in the correct order. He liked computers – especially programming, of which he had done a little. Whereas Katy Kite was much more laid back and was always chasing some fascinating idea, Pixel Pete preferred to take life step by step and in the right order. He tended to keep himself to himself.

Katy Kite and Pixel Pete had their own living space in a large open-plan room in the middle of the mansion, and their corners of the room looked quite different from each other. Katy Kite's corner was, er, . . . quite untidy. It did not matter to her that everything was all over the floor. She loved the rambling feeling of her space, with its creative pictures and dreamy music that helped her relax. She did admit that it was sometimes difficult to find things – they tended to wander off like she did. Her ceiling was painted blue with white clouds.

The Amazing Tale of the
Mysterious Magical Mansion page 4

On the other hand, in Pixel Pete's corner everything was always in the right place. He was neat and tidy. He had 'Things to do' lists on the wall and all his books were carefully placed on the shelves. He liked everything in order and always noticed when things were not in place. All his clothes were folded. His bed was made and his shoes were neatly put under the bed *and* polished.

Katy Kite and Pixel Pete liked to spend time by themselves and get on with life in their own way. But sometimes they worked and played together. Together, they discovered that they could do more than either of them could do alone. Even though they were so different in character, together they matched up and made up for each other like real friends. When Pixel Pete couldn't imagine as widely as Katy Kite could, for example, Katy Kite imagined for him. When Katy Kite couldn't organise as well as Pixel Pete, Pixel Pete organised for her. Together, they were a real team. Together, they were versatile.

They realised that they had their own talents and gifts, and that together they were more talented and gifted. Sometimes they surprised themselves by what they achieved. They became powerful.

There are two more characters in the Magical Mansion. We shall meet them later!

The Characters Pixel Pete and Katy Kite

➤ Draw the twins. Use the rest of the space to record your thoughts about Pixel Pete and Katy Kite. You might want to think about what each of them look like, their character, their strengths and how they like to do things. Draw the Magical Mansion on the back.

Pixel Pete

Katy Kite

Your Room

➤ Let's take a minute to think about your room. What does your room say about you?

Maybe your room shows your hidden personality?

What do you think? Discuss this idea with someone. Find out what they think.

Now think in more detail about your room and what it is like. Maybe you would like to bring in a photograph of it and stick it on the back.

Who does your room say you are more like? Pixel Pete or Katy Kite?

Mark an 'X' on the line below to indicate where your room shows you to be.

I am more like:

Pixel Pete

Katy Kite

Why do you think you placed yourself at this point between Katy Kite and Pixel Pete?

The Magical Mansion Gang: the Twins

➤ Pixel Pete and Katy Kite take two different approaches to study.

Pixel Pete
Goes for the detail.

He is an analytical thinker. He is logical, he wants to know the facts, and he is neat and tidy and keeps himself to himself. He carries a magnifying glass in his right hand so that he can focus on the details.

Katy Kite
Rises to new perspectives.

Katy is insightful. She is good at looking at matters from a different perspective to seek out patterns and connections. She likes spotting the broad themes and big ideas. She thinks in a holistic way. She is philosophical and good at writing poems on the themes she finds. She is a dreamer, left-handed, expressive and rather laid back. She loves her baggy clothes, which help her to feel free.

Pixel Pete and Katy Kite are close friends as well as twins, but sometimes they drive each other mad! However, when they work well together, they make a versatile team and can tackle any challenge as they complement each other's strengths.

1.5

My *RSG!* Learning Log

➤ Use at least three of the following prompts to record your thoughts on today's studio session:

● Today I learned ....
....
....
....

● The most useful thing I will take from today is ....
....
....
....

● I was surprised by ....
....
....
....

● I was interested in ....
....
....
....

● What I liked most was ....
....
....
....

● One thing I'm not sure about is ....
....
....
....

● The main thing I want to find out more about is ....
....
....
....

● After today I feel ....
....
....
....

● I might have got more from today if ....
....
....
....

INSIDE YOUR OWN MAGICAL MANSION

■ APPROACH

This simple task has repeatedly proved to be most valuable in helping pupils think about how they think and how others think. Drawing the inside of their own Magical Mansion, the interiority of their mind, produces some wonderful results.

Many pupils create beautiful drawings (using A3) which often contain hugely interesting insights into their inner worlds – see the examples on the next page. The drawings often prompt powerful conversations about study. As an example, one child drew an attic in her mansion. It was a very small attic and right at the top of her head. There was a ladder leading to the hatch. The ladder had two broken rungs. The attic was the perfection room at the top of her mansion. She knew that she would probably never reach it, but it was there to aim for. Another pupil also had a perfection room. She wrote: 'The smallest room in my brain is a little perfect room right at the top of my head. This perfect room is so small that no one knows it is there.'

■ ACTION

➤ 1 Game: Mansion Daydream

Resources CD player and relaxing classical music.

Aim To enhance imagination skills and encourage self-evaluation.

What to do The pupils sit or lie with their eyes closed while you play a piece of music. This time, ask them to imagine a scene in which they are walking through their own Magical Mansion, peering into the different rooms inside their head. Invite them to walk down the corridors, noticing the lighting, the windows, and the contents inside the rooms – by which they know which room it is. A happiness room might include some objects from a special holiday, or something a friend gave them. They can show these in their drawing later.

INSIDE YOUR OWN MAGICAL MANSION

➤ 2 Draw your own Magical Mansion

Resources A3 paper and colouring pens/pencils for each pupil.

Ask the pupils to remember how the rooms in the Magical Mansion worked – there was no limit to what you could put in a room, and some rooms were forgotten or unused. Tell them to draw their own Magical Mansion. They can put anything in there from a small toy to something huge. Encourage them to let their imaginations have full reign. Check that they know they are drawing their own head and not making one up. (Making one up, would, in itself, be a starting point for a very useful conversation.)

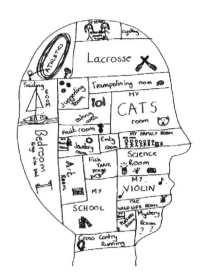 

Ask the pupils to leave one room empty – a mystery room. The pupils need to do this for Conversation 3. The room does not need to be big – just a location that they can zoom in on and draw separately later.

- Ask the pupils questions about the features in their rooms to find out more.

- Ask them to show you their favourite room and explain why it is their favourite.

- Ask them to share their Magical Mansion drawings with each other.

- Pair them up with their friends and with those who are not necessarily their friends to learn what each of them is thinking about. This is particularly valuable for understanding a little better someone they don't normally sit beside.

A blank template of a head is provided (Photocopiable 2.1, page 40) for those pupils who would like to start with an outline drawing.

■ APPRAISAL

Display the pupils' drawings of their Magical Mansions.

They like to talk about their personal drawings, show them to others and have them on display. When they are older, they enjoy remembering their Magical Mansion drawings. They love to draw one a year later and then look back on what they saw inside their head when they were younger. This visual mnemonic powerfully supports and models metacognition and self-evaluation.

➤ The *RSG!* Round: Making 'I' contact

See Conversation 1, page 29.

WHAT IS STUDY?

■ APPROACH

We now leave the Magical Mansion for a while. The third conversation focuses on discussion, questions and answers. Through these what the pupils already think and feel about study will begin to surface. This is a useful benchmarking exercise against which to measure progress and changes in points of view at a later stage.

The main aim of this first full discussion session in the studio is to create an atmosphere in which the pupils feel safe to offer to each other their underlying attitudes to study. You can encourage them to become aware of and practise explaining what they are really thinking. Welcome the negative comments as well as the positive ones. Try to instil an atmosphere of 'unconditional positive regard' (see page 19). Some pupils will be hard pushed to produce any positive comments. That is the point of this course! Value what they say even if it is negative because bringing the negative thoughts to the surface makes it possible to examine and modify them through conversation – they may hear some positive ways of looking at study from their peers. This may begin to open up, in their own minds, new ways of seeing aspects of study which they have previously thought to be bad.

■ ACTION

➤ 1 Questions

- Ask the pupils to complete the exercise 'What Do you Think?' (Photocopiable 3.1, page 42). Allocate questions to different groups and get them to report their answers back to the class.

- The pupils can record their understanding in any way they feel appropriate: bullet points, key words, pictures, symbols, colours.

- Follow up with discussion in pairs, in groups, and as a whole class with you.

- They can add new points that arise in the discussion to their own answers.

➤ 2 Your Mystery Room

Using 'The Mystery Room' (Photocopiable 3.2, page 43), ask the pupils to draw an enlargement of the Mystery Room which they included in the drawing they did in Conversation 2.

This is their study. This is the place where they keep their inmost thoughts on school and study, homework, revision, class – all the aspects of life in school that combine to help make them better students.

Ask them to express their thinking. What do they find in their study?

■ APPRAISAL

➤ The *RSG!* Round: Making 'I' contact

See Conversation 1, page 29.

What Do you Think?

➤ What pictures, ideas or words come into your head when someone says 'study' to you? Write or draw some of them in the box below.

Some questions to help you in your thinking:

- What is study?

- What kind of *actions* does study involve?

- What kind of *thinking* does study involve?

- What kind of *feelings* do you have when you think of study?

- What parts of study do you like?

- Does study only happen in school?

- Who studies?

- Whom do you study for?

➤ Now share your ideas and thoughts. Add any new ones below.

© *ReadyStudyGo!* LDA   Permission to Photocopy

The Mystery Room

➤ It's your study! What's in it?

IN YOUR STRIDE!

■ APPROACH

The idea of a developmental journey underpins this course and highlights the value for each pupil of building an attitudinal approach and the determination to travel independently as a student.

Research has shown that the 'deep' students take study in their stride. They know their strengths and limits. They know where they are overreaching. They know where they are going. They have goals. (For more information on this, see page 10.) Vygotsky's (1978) work on the Zone of Proximal Development is relevant here.

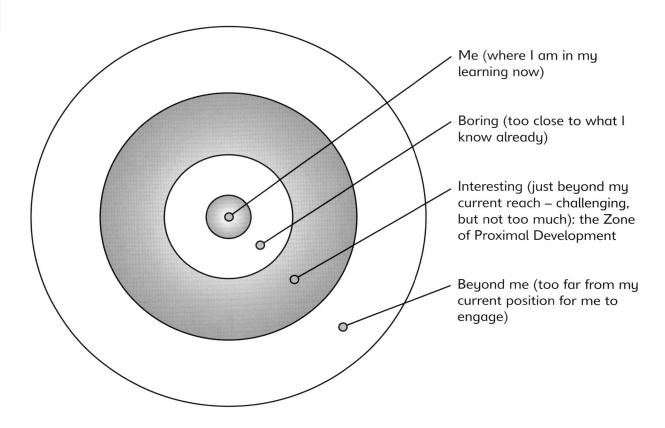

Me (where I am in my learning now)

Boring (too close to what I know already)

Interesting (just beyond my current reach – challenging, but not too much): the Zone of Proximal Development

Beyond me (too far from my current position for me to engage)

Small steps away from the current position can be boring for a pupil, and aiming for a destination too far away for a personal stride length can lead to demotivation – literally a stopping of moving forward in learning. The capacity to manage their movement implies a high level of self-knowledge on the part of the pupil about what they can take in their stride. Let's work at this idea through some physical movement.

This studio conversation is designed to be reassuring. Taking study in your stride has negative connotations for most pupils. The conversation encourages them to reflect on how they can best match their study habits to their own personal stride length (which will be different from someone else's stride) and to think about where they are going in a deeper sense. You may decide to split the session into two or more parts to make sure pupils fully explore the issues.

IN YOUR STRIDE!

▪ ACTION

➤ 1   Questions

- Do you know what 'taking it in your stride' means?

- Can you demonstrate short and long strides, as well as easy, comfortable and strenuous strides? Note that this will depend on their personal preference – which offers a way of stepping into the idea of personalised learning.

- Compare two different pupils – a stride is long for one and short for the other.

- Mark out their stride lengths on the floor. Ask them to work in pairs and measure and record their stride length on 'My Stride' (Photocopiable 4.1, page 49).

- Notice the differences, particularly that a strenuous stride for one pupil may be easy for another.

- What can we do when we feel we are 'outside our stride'?

- Where are you going (in terms of school work and personally)?

➤ 2   Worksheet

- Complete the questions on the worksheet 'My Stride' in pairs. Discuss your answers in groups.

➤ 3   Game: Imaginary Journey

Resources None.

Aim To explore the idea of a journey inside your head.

What to do Ask the pupils to make a large circle. Explain that they are going on a journey. They are to act out what happens and try to imagine the three H's – how they think, feel and act – as they are going.

- They have to complete an obstacle course.

- They have to cross a meadow set with traps.

Make the ideas and thoughts relevant to study. What are the traps and snares – the obstacles that arise in studying?

After many difficulties, they reach their destination.

Bring the children back together and discuss what they learned about their thinking during this activity.

IN YOUR STRIDE!

➤ 4   Worksheet

•   Complete 'Setting out on a Journey' (Photocopiable 4.2, page 50). Explain that the mnemonic STRIDE leads to six questions that provide a useful series of footholds for the young traveller in the learning landscape; 'Stride' (see Photocopiable 4.3, page 51).

Work through each of the descriptions, questions and activities on Photocopiables 4.4–4.9 (pages 52–57). You may want to take more than one session to do this. A brief description of each foothold is given below.

➤ S is for Starting

Successful students can get started when they need to (e.g. for a lesson or homework), in a group or on their own.

Here is a tip to help them kick-start themselves into beginning. It is not always easy to do this. They should take each new time when they don't feel like starting as an opportunity to get better. It is possible to overcome this particular barrier by sticking at it. The trick is to tune the brain into lighting up just one or two relevant networks. This can be done in the simplest way by looking at the smallest fact or idea, old or new, and thinking 'What do I know about this? What does it make me think of?' The brain will take notice if they keep trying to focus on that thinking. Small steps lead to progress.

➤ T is for Teaching

Successful students are their own best teachers. They recognise what helps them study and notice what their favourite teachers do so that they can do it for themselves.

➤ R is for Reflecting

Successful students make new information relevant to themselves. They look for links and connections to what they know already, new ideas, fun ideas, patterns. Most important of all, they can make the material interesting to them personally. They work out why it might be relevant and aren't easily put off if it seems irrelevant at first. They know that if they can master it, it helps them along the way on their journey. That makes everything relevant! They think about any new learning they are doing. They watch others working and reflect on how they approach the same task differently and what they might do differently to help themselves.

➤ I is for Imagining

Successful students are imaginative in the way they study. They invent ways of seeing new information unusually in order to appeal to their imagination. They invent stories and think up ways of making the information memorable. For example, they might imagine themselves as a red blood cell in the blood stream. What would that be like? What would they have to think, feel and do to be a red blood cell?

➤ D is for Discussing

Successful students chat with friends about their work. Turning new ideas into conversations with a friend or group of friends often improves ideas and sometimes generates more ideas and better understanding. Listening to others explaining their ideas about the same topic

IN YOUR STRIDE!

helps you to improve your ideas and to remember. Discussing helps to fit new information into your brain networks. Students who discuss are good at expressing their own ideas, finding out about what others think, sharing and explaining their thinking. They are also good at listening to what others say and saying something in return that helps the other person move their thinking on.

> ➤ E is for Evaluating

To evaluate means to bring out what is valuable about something. Successful students think back over successes and failures and learn from them to get closer to more success. They dig for the nugget of gold, no matter how small. These students have developed a 'thick skin' and learn from their mistakes rather than giving up. They can take a few knocks. They are always on the look-out for ways to get better. They understand that failing can be turned into new learning and that it moves them closer to getting it right next time. Getting something wrong (which we all do sometimes) does not make them feel bad for long. And they never give up, even when the going gets tough. They watch and evaluate others working, and reflect on how someone else approaches the same task differently and what they might do differently to help themselves.

They can see where the value is in what they did – what worked and is therefore valuable – and what didn't work and is not valuable, yet open for improvement.

▪ APPRAISAL

- Ask the pupils to think about the last time they felt good about a piece of work. What did they do that made it successful? How can they repeat that formula to achieve success?

- Ask them to think about the last time they did not do something well at school. What did they do or not do that made it go wrong?

- In groups of six to eight, get them to talk about what they would do differently now that they have evaluated their failure by looking back and learning.

- Again in a group, ask them to discuss if they have ever turned a failure into a success. What did they do? Get them to evaluate their actions.

- In pairs, get the pupils to consider how they can become even better at finding the gold in the future.

- They should ask their partner to help them think about this.

- Encourage them to write down individually two or three actions to try later.

Explain that if they can't bring a success or failure to mind easily, they should avoid thinking too big or being too hard on themselves. Sometimes the tiniest little success or failure is all they need to evaluate in order to see ways of bringing more success for themselves. Often, we find it easy to think of when we failed big-time, and hard to think of the tiniest success. This is a natural human reaction. But all successes, no matter how small, are nuggets of gold. We tend to ignore success for some reason, and we have a reaction to failure that makes it bigger than it is. We explore this idea further in Conversation 8.

IN YOUR STRIDE!

➤ The *RSG!* Round: Making 'I' contact

See Conversation 1, page 29.

➤ Round: 'Something I have achieved is . . . '

Resources None.

Aim To celebrate achievement and set up goals.

What to do The pupils sit in an inward-facing circle. In turn they finish the sentence 'Something I have achieved is . . . '. They could repeat this with the sentence 'The next achievement I am aiming for is . . . '. You might want to warn children beforehand in case some need time and encouragement to think of an achievement. The smallest achievement counts.

My Stride

➤ Work in pairs.

● A stride is . . . .

● The length of my stride is:

Short . . . . cm

Normal . . . . cm

Long . . . . cm

Biggest . . . . cm

● When do I use the different lengths of stride?. . . . .
. . . .
. . . .
. . . .

When I take strides of different lengths:

● What am I thinking? . . . .
. . . .
. . . .
. . . .

● What am I doing? . . . .
. . . .
. . . .
. . . .

● What am I feeling? . . . .
. . . .
. . . .
. . . .

Setting out on a Journey

● Where will my studies lead me? . . . .
. . . .
. . . .

● Where do I want to go? . . . .
. . . .
. . . .

● What stride lengths will I need to get there? . . . .
. . . .
. . . .

● Why should I bother to study in class? . . . .
. . . .
. . . .

● Why should I bother to do my homework? . . . .
. . . .
. . . .

● Who am I doing all this for? . . . .
. . . .
. . . .

When I get where I want to go:

● What shall I be thinking? . . . .
. . . .
. . . .

● What shall I be doing? . . . .
. . . .
. . . .

● What shall I be feeling? . . . .
. . . .
. . . .

Stride

➤ STRIDE gives you six questions to ask yourself and to keep coming back to.

S *Starting* How can I get better at starting to study?

T *Teaching* How can I be my own best teacher?

R *Reflecting* How can I reflect and make new things feel relevant and not boring?

I *Imagining* What story, or pictures, or events can I imagine to help me remember this information?

D *Discussing* With whom shall I discuss what I have learned?

E *Evaluating* What did I do well and what could I do better next time?

S is for Starting

➤ Successful students can start when they need. They ask: 'How can I get started?'

Questions:
● Think of some examples of people who are good at getting started. Who are they? . . .
....
....

● How do athletes prepare to start a race? ....
....
....

● What stories have you read about people who are or were good starters? ....
....
....

● Why is it a good idea to start well in a lesson or get started on homework? ....
....
....

Three H's check:
● What do people who are good at starting do? ....
....
....

● How do they think? ....
....
....

● What do they feel? ....
....
....

Self-check:
● Think about a task you are finding it difficult to start.
● How would it help you if you did start? ....
....
....

● How can you be an even better starter? ....
....
....

● Ask a partner to help you think about this. Write down two or three actions to try
later. ....
....
....

4.5

T is for Teaching

➤ Successful students are their own best teachers. They ask: 'How can I best support myself?'

Questions:
● Who is/are your favourite teacher(s)? . . . .
. . . .
. . . .

● Why are they your favourite teacher(s)? . . . .
. . . .
. . . .

● What do they do that you like? . . . .
. . . .
. . . .

● Make a note of the things they do that help you to study and make progress . . . . . .
. . . .
. . . .

● Three H's check:
What do people who are good at teaching do? . . . .
. . . .
. . . .

● How do they think? . . . .
. . . .
. . . .

● What do they feel? . . . .
. . . .
. . . .

Self-check:
● How can you be a good teacher to yourself? . . . .
. . . .
. . . .

● Ask a partner to help you think about this.
● Write down two or three actions to try later. . . . .
. . . .
. . . .

R is for Reflecting

➤ Successful students make new information relevant to themselves. They ask: 'How could this be interesting?'

Questions:
● Whom do you know who is good at reflecting on what they do? . . . .
. . . .
. . . .

● What characters from history or books, or TV or cartoons, can you think of who are really strong at reflecting on what they do? . . . .
. . . .
. . . .

Three H's check:
● What do people who are good at reflection do? . . . .
. . . .
. . . .

● How do they think? . . . .
. . . .
. . . .

● What do they feel? . . . .
. . . .
. . . .

Self-check:
● How might you become more reflective as a student? . . . .
. . . .
. . . .

● Ask a partner to help you think about this.
● Write down two or three actions to try later. . . . .
. . . .
. . . .
. . . .

I is for Imagining

➤ Successful students are imaginative in the way they study. They say: 'Let my brain go!'

Questions:

● Whom do you know who is good with their imagination? . . . .
. . . .
. . . .

● What characters from history or books, or TV or cartoons, can you think of who are really strong at being imaginative? . . . .
. . . .
. . . .

Three H's check:

● What do people who are good at imagining do? . . . .
. . . .
. . . .

● How do they think? . . . .
. . . .
. . . .

● What do they feel? . . . .
. . . .
. . . .

Self-check:

● How can you use imagination in study? . . . .
. . . .
. . . .

● Ask a partner to help you think about this.
● Write down two or three actions to try later. . . . .
. . . .
. . . .
. . . .

D is for Discussing

➤ Successful students talk with friends about their work. They know: 'It's good to talk!'

Questions:

● Whom do you know who is good at discussing what they have learned or what they know? . . . .
. . . .
. . . .

● What characters from history or books, or TV or cartoons, can you think of who are really strong at discussion? . . . .
. . . .
. . . .

Three H's check:

● What do people who are good at discussion do? . . . .
. . . .
. . . .

● How do they think? . . . .
. . . .
. . . .

● What do they feel? . . . .
. . . .
. . . .

Self-check:

● How can you take even more part in discussions? . . . .
. . . .
. . . .

● Ask a partner to help you think about this.
● Write down two or three actions to try later. . . . .
. . . .
. . . .
. . . .

E is for Evaluating

➤ Successful students find the gold from how well they did or didn't do last time. They say: 'Look back and learn!'

Questions:
● Whom do you know who is good at looking back on what was successful and doing even better next time? . . . .
. . . .
. . . .

● Whom do you know who can do that when they are *not* successful? . . . .
. . . .
. . . .

● What characters from history or books, or TV or cartoons, can you think of who are really strong at finding value in what they and others do? . . . .
. . . .
. . . .

Three H's check:
● What do people who are good at evaluating do? . . . .
. . . .
. . . .

● How do they think? . . . .
. . . .
. . . .

● What do they feel? . . . .
. . . .
. . . .

Self-check:
● How can you evaluate what you do? . . . .
. . . .
. . . .

● Ask a partner to help you to think about this.
● Write down two or three actions to try later. . . . .
. . . .
. . . .
. . . .

PREFERENCES

■ APPROACH

This conversation taps into kinaesthetic learning to introduce the idea of preference. It sets up the thinking of the pupils, in advance, on the different personal learning style distinctions that are the main purpose of the Magical Mansion Gang. The aim here is to sensitise the pupils, at a subtle level, to the power of their physical and sensory strengths through a greater awareness of their mind–body connections. You may wish to link this lesson with Brain Gym® (see www.braingym.org and www.learning-solutions.co.uk) or PE or other physical sessions in music and movement or drama.

Be sensitive to those pupils who are vulnerable to a discussion on limbs and the experience of physically touching and sensing the world on account of their personal or family medical history.

The pupils' attention is drawn to the subtlety of fine-motor control and the feelings that accompany the individual and combined use of their left and right hands and limbs. It is designed to model their understanding of different learning preferences.

Pupils explore the strengths that lie in difference – valuing each other's perspective. This is an opportunity to celebrate the special capabilities of left-handed pupils, who may sometimes feel that they are different.

■ ACTION

➤ 1 Left hand, right hand

Set up some simple exercises to help the pupils compare their right- and left-handedness:

- Throwing a soft ball to someone with each hand separately.

- Writing their name with each hand.

- Folding their arms. Which hand is on top? Now ask them to try it the other way.

Emphasise that they are both right- and left-handed all of the time, but that most people have a preference.

- What does it feel like to be 'working outside your preferences'?

➤ 2 Both hands

Talk about ambidextrous capabilities.

- Do any of the pupils think they are indecisive sometimes about which hand to use?

- Do any of the pupils play a musical instrument involving both hands? If so, ask if they will demonstrate for the rest to watch. Discuss whether there is a musical instrument that is played with one hand only.

- Ask if anyone can juggle. Again, encourage a demonstration. This is a good example of using both hands carefully.

- Find out if anyone can use a diabolo. As before, try to get them to give a demonstration.

- Ask for other examples of two-handedness.

PREFERENCES

> ➤ 3 Feet

Finally, ask the pupils to explore the idea of preference in terms of their feet. They can discuss what they discover about themselves. Skateboarders, snowboarders and surfers will know the terms 'switch' and 'goofy', which refer to someone who stands on the board 'the other way'.

Explore what each pupil's dominant foot is (if they have one):

* Ask them to lean forwards without moving their feet. As they pass the point of balance, their instinct will be to shoot out a foot to save themselves from falling. This will be their dominant foot.

* Ask them to imagine they are on a surfboard and to put their strong foot at the front. Now get them to go 'switch'.

* Ask them to imagine they are walking up steps quickly. Which foot goes first? Is it usually the same one?

* Ask them to kick a soft ball with each foot separately and think about how it feels.

* Do they think their ability to use each foot would get better with practice?

Ask the pupils to make up their own ways of testing their laterality.

APPRAISAL

> ➤ Feeling and awareness – body feedback

Now that the pupils have established that they are often more comfortable using one or other of their hands or feet for any particular task, they can become more aware of their ability to feel and to sense objects, to enjoy textures and surfaces, and so on. This is equally relevant to their hands and feet and always applies (unless they have experienced an accident or are under the influence of anaesthesia).

* Ask the pupils to close their eyes and describe a range of materials you and they have gathered.

* Get them to identify the materials.

* Encourage them to use their hands to help them.

* Now suggest that they use their bare feet.

This activity underlines that although almost all of us think of ourselves as left- or right-handed, both hands are working all the time, each supporting the other without really knowing it. Each is as much 'alive' as the other. This is the grounding for understanding the analytical and holist learning approaches embodied in Pixel Pete and Katy Kite.

> ➤ Round: 'I prefer . . . to . . . '

Resources None.

Aim To explore individual preferences.

What to do The pupils sit in an inward-facing circle. Each pupil declares a preference they have, such as 'I prefer jam to peanut butter', 'I prefer hot to cold'.

> ➤ The *RSG!* Round: Making 'I' contact

See Conversation 1 (page 29).

CHARACTERISTICS

▪ APPROACH

This conversation explores the words 'character' and 'characteristics'. The pupils will be thinking about the characteristics of the characters in the story at some length in the conversations that follow this one.

▪ ACTION

➤ 1 Game: Ten Circles

Resources A3 paper and pencils.

Aim To help pupils think about and appreciate the differences between people.

What to do Give each child a piece of A3 paper and a pencil. Ask them to draw ten circles. Some will ask for more instructions. There is none. Ask them to get up and look at everyone's version. What do they notice? Most children will have done something different.

Now ask them to sit down and look at their neighbour's ten circles. They should tell their neighbour what they think they have drawn (a ladybird close up, planets . . .). Again they will notice that they have different ideas.

Next ask them to draw ten circles again, but this time ask them to do something creative with their circles. Encourage them to get up and look at everyone else's.

➤ 2 Questions

- Talk together about what characteristics are.

- Where do somebody's characteristics come from? (They could discuss upbringing, genes, the genome project, etc.).

- How can you tell which are the good and the bad characters in a play?

- Can you tell the character of different animals? What behaviours are involved?

- Do you agree amongst yourselves about what you learned through considering characteristics?

➤ 3 Analysis

- Point out that there are three key words inside the word 'characteristics': 'character', 'act' and 'I' – how 'I act' shows my 'character' to others.

- What do you think your characteristics are?

- How do others see you?

- Complete the worksheet 'My Characteristics' (Photocopiable 6.1, page 62). Explain that the pupils should ask their friends for help.

CHARACTERISTICS

➤ 4 Game: Knowing Me, Knowing You

Resources CD player, recording of ABBA's 'Knowing Me, Knowing You' in the album *Arrival* (1976) and in *ABBA Gold: Greatest Hits* (1992).

Aim To explore the characteristics of classmates.

What to do Play 'Knowing Me, Knowing You'. In pairs, the pupils think of three likes or dislikes, preferences or characteristics – only one of which is true. Each pupil has to decide which one is true for their partner. Once both have had a turn, get them to find new partners and repeat.

■ APPRAISAL

➤ Other activities

Resources Recording of TV play (check in advance whether the pupils have already seen the play).

- Discuss the characteristics of some TV characters.

- Play a recording showing characters in a TV play they have not seen and ask them to evaluate the people on the basis of their actions in very short extracts.

- Play a game in which you think of a character for the pupils to discover. They ask questions which are answered by 'Yes' or 'No'.

➤ Round: 'I like . . . '

Resources None.

Aim To help pupils start to think about and appreciate the differences between people.

What to do Each child in turn finishes the sentence 'I like . . .'. They may say a favourite food, hobby or item of clothing, but not people. The other pupils put their hand up after each turn if they agree.

➤ The *RSG!* Round: Making 'I' contact

See Conversation 1 (page 29).

Having focused the pupils' thinking on characters and characteristics, return their minds to the two characters introduced in the story so far and build up a list of the characteristics of Pixel Pete and Katy Kite on the worksheet provided (Photocopiable 6.2, page 63), working individually, in pairs and in groups.

My Characteristics

➤ Get a few friends to help you to write your list. They can write in the box below. Then help them do their list.

Name:

6.2

Pixel Pete's and Katy Kite's Characteristics

➤ Let's get to know Pixel Pete and Katy Kite!

Write down things that describe Pixel Pete's character:

_____

_____

_____

_____

_____

_____

_____

_____

_____

_____

_____

_____

_____

_____

_____

_____

_____

Write down things that describe Katy Kite's character:

_____

_____

_____

_____

_____

_____

_____

_____

_____

_____

_____

_____

_____

_____

_____

_____

_____

Now, think again: which character are you more like?
(draw an X on the line)

Pixel Pete ——————————————————————— **Katy Kite**

PIXEL PETE AND KATY KITE

■ APPROACH

This conversation asks the pupils to revisit the Magical Mansion and to think about and discuss the first two characters in the story. There are two worksheets for them to use to record what they remember and think about the twins. This is not a memory test, but a record of what has struck them – a useful indication of their inner thinking.

■ ACTION

➤ 1 Game: Take my hand

Resources None.

Aim An enjoyable starter exercise to get children moving.

What to do The pupils form an inward-facing circle. The teacher says a number below 10. The pupils have to hold hands in groups of the specified number, if necessary moving to do so. Any children left can form up into a smaller group.

➤ 2 Discussion

Discuss the preferences and characteristics of the twins on the basis of the work of the previous sessions.

➤ 3 Complete the worksheet for each character

Ask the pupils to complete the worksheets for the two characters (Photocopiables 7.1 and 7.2, pages 67–68). Value the ideas they produce and congratulate them on their thinking. There are no right and wrong answers in terms of what they think – because that's what they think. It is this thinking that you want to get a picture of in order to explore their approach to study.

- Ask the pupils to complete the task individually, entering a few key words or ideas in the boxes.

- Ask them to talk these through with a partner and share ideas.

- Now, in groups of four, ask them to come up with some ideas about why these characteristics are strengths. What would this person do for their friends? What advantages would there be in knowing them?

- Then take feedback from the class.

- You could complete each character's page on a whiteboard or flipchart and then discuss your findings, especially the strengths.

■ APPRAISAL

➤ 1 Round: 'I like . . . '

Resources None.

Aim To help pupils start to think about and appreciate the differences between the characters of Pixel Pete and Katy Kite.

PIXEL PETE AND KATY KITE

What to do Divide the pupils so that half pretend to be Pixel Pete and the rest Katy Kite. In turn, alternating between Pixel Pete and Katy Kite, ask a volunteer to finish the sentence, 'I like . . .'. They can include favourite foods, hobbies or clothes, but not people. The other pupils can put their hand up after each turn if they like the same thing.

➤ 2 The twins help me

Resources None.

Aim To reflect on how the two characters could help pupils tackle a particular challenge or learning task.

What to do Ask the pupils to sit in a circle facing each other. In turn, they complete each of the following sentences: 'Pixel Pete would help me by . . .', 'Katy Kite would help me by . . .'.

➤ 3   The *RSG!* Round: Making 'I' contact

See Conversation 1 (page 29).

➤ 4 Extension activities

Use the poem that follows to start a conversation and some other creative work.

> *The Two-sided Man*
>
> Much I owe to the lands that grew –
>
> More to the Lives that fed –
>
> But most to Allah Who gave me two
>
> Separate sides to my head.
>
> Much I reflect on the Good and the True
>
> In the Faiths beneath the sun
>
> But most upon Allah Who gave me the two
>
> Sides of my head, not one.
>
> I would go without shirt or shoe,
>
> Friend, tobacco or bread,
>
> Sooner than lose for a minute the two
>
> Separate sides of my head!

Rudyard Kipling

PIXEL PETE AND KATY KITE

Or use this story.

Thomas Gladwin, an anthropologist, contrasted the ways in which a European and a native Turkese sailor navigate small boats between tiny islands in the vast Pacific Ocean:

> Before setting sail, the European begins with a plan that can be written in terms of directions, degrees of longitude and latitude, estimated time of arrival at separate points on a journey. Once the plan is conceived and completed, the sailor has only to carry out each step consecutively, one after another, to be assured of arriving on time at the planned destination. The sailor uses all available tools, such as a compass, a sextant, a map etc. and, if asked, can describe exactly how he got where he was going.

> In contrast, the native Turkese sailor starts his voyage by imagining the position of his destination relative to the position of the other islands. As he sails along, he constantly adjusts his direction according to his awareness of his position thus far. His decisions are improvised continually by checking relative positions of landmarks, sun, wind direction etc. He navigates with reference to where he started, where he is going, and the space between his destination and the point where he is at the moment. If asked how he navigates so well without instruments or a written plan, he cannot possibly put it into words. This is not because the Turkese are unaccustomed to describing things in words, but rather because the process is too complex and fluid to be put into words. (*Paredes and Hepburn* 1976)

Pixel Pete: Someone who Goes for the Detail

➤ Think of someone you know who is like Pixel Pete. If you can't think of someone you know, then think of a comic, cartoon, film or TV character – or even an animal – who makes you think of him.

● How do you know they are like Pixel Pete? What do they do and say that makes you think they are a logical thinker? How do they act? Write a few ideas in the box below.

● Now, think very carefully. Why are these characteristics *strengths*?

● Discuss your ideas with someone else and write down some new ideas.

● Record all the things you have found out in class about your friends and characters who are like Pixel Pete.

Katy Kite: Someone who Goes for the Big Story

➤ Think of someone you know who is like Katy Kite. If you can't think of someone you know, then think of a comic, cartoon, film or TV character – or even an animal – who makes you think of her.

● How do you know they are like Katy Kite? What do they do and say that makes you think they are a creative thinker? How do they act? Write a few ideas in the box below.

● Now, think very carefully. Why are these characteristics *strengths*?

● Discuss your ideas with someone else and write down some new ideas.

● Record all the things you have found out in class about your friends and characters who are like Katy Kite.

Permission to Photocopy

SEEING IS BELIEVING!

■ APPROACH

This conversation is supported by the use of optical illusions. It is linked with the thinking on preferences that has been introduced in Conversation 5. It also introduces the idea that things are not always what they seem to be, which is an important insight when a student is facing a fear.

■ ACTION

Present and discuss the optical illusions on the worksheet (Photocopiable 8.1, page 73).

In 'seeing' the pictures on the worksheet, the pupils will notice how they naturally and very quickly pick up the dominant image for them – one of the two ways of seeing the diagram will be immediately apparent. That represents a preference. They then have to work to disconnect their serialist brain, which wants to hold on to that image (now that it is analysed), and ask their brain to make a switch. This shows that we can work outside our preferences and that it is possible to be versatile.

Optical illusions

➤ Face or vase?

The pupils will tend to see one version immediately, and will find it easy to see the other possibility.

➤ Duck or rabbit?

The second illustration supplied may appear as either a duck with its beak to the upper left corner, or as a rabbit with its ears in that corner.

➤ Schroeder's stairs

Most pupils will probably see the staircase from above as if they are looking at the footmarks by looking down on it. Ask them to concentrate on viewing the image from underneath, so that the two footsteps seem to be above them.

If the pupils find the switch difficult, suggest that they try:

- blinking;

- focusing on one of the upper corners (this often works);

- sending the side of the staircase either to the front or the back depending on which version they see first;

- covering up the horizontal line at the base of the drawing.

Ask them to notice their feelings as they make the swap. Tell them not to worry if they don't see the swap at first; it comes with time and patience.

➤ 1 Points for discussion

- Notice that both versions of the drawings on the worksheet exist, but you can only focus on one at once.

SEEING IS BELIEVING!

- I have found it helpful for the pupils to think of their preferences as operating all the time, but with one predominating to start with. With a little effort, they can bring more of the less dominant characteristics 'to mind'. They can become more aware, as they did in Conversation 5 by thinking about their hands and feet, of how sensibilities operate continuously, even though they have a preference which determines some aspects of their own personal characteristics.

➤ 2 Questions

Encourage the pupils to discuss the questions on the worksheet, which carry on from their consideration of the optical illusions. Discuss their thoughts.

➤ 3 Game: What is it?

Resources Everyday objects.

Bring a range of objects into the class or ask the pupils to collect items. These are everyday objects. The idea is to put the objects on the floor in the middle of a circle of standing pupils. They then look at what is available (e.g. sponge, spoon, colander, shoe horn) and take turns to explain what one is and what it is for - as long as it is not the normal use. A sponge might be a 'Finger-muscle trainer' (to be squeezed and released while being held in one hand); the spoon might be an 'eye strengthener' (putting the spoon to one eye and looking purposefully round the room with the other); the colander might become an 'alien signal-receiving helmet' (putting it on the head and making beeping noises while pretending to adjust the helmet at the side); the shoe horn might be a slide for ants.

Encourage as much creative, even wacky, thinking as possible. This is an investigation of how objects can become something else.

➤ 4 Game: The Troll's Treasure

Resources Large cardboard box or other container to represent a treasure chest.

Aim To introduce the theme of overcoming fears.

What to do The pupils sit in a large inward-facing circle. Choose a child to be the troll and tell them they need to guard the treasure chest, which is placed on the floor inside the circle and near the troll somewhere. The pupils are numbered 1–5. When the teacher calls a number from 1 to 5, the pupils with that number enter the circle. They try to grab the treasure and return to their place without the troll touching them. Any child who is touched must return to their chair.

➤ 5 Facing fears

Sometimes things appear to us to be worse than they really are. This is often felt by pupils who are facing new challenges. It may feel as if the threat is much larger than it really is. To support a discussion on this idea, you can use the following story.

SEEING IS BELIEVING!

The Young Hero and the Giant

Once upon a time there was a young traveller who journeyed through foreign lands seeking enlightenment and truth. One evening he arrived at a small hamlet in a steep valley with a dark forest beyond. As he arrived, people looked at him with disbelief. He stopped one of the inhabitants and asked the reason for such strange looks. The villager told him that he had arrived in the hamlet at the worst possible time in the year. Tomorrow was the day. 'The day for what?' he asked.

'The day the giant comes.'

He was taken aback. 'The giant?'

He learned from the terrified villager that once a year, for nearly twenty years, on the same day of the same month, a fearsome giant strode out of the dark forest (which no one dared enter at any time) and demanded to do battle with the bravest and best warrior in the village. And every year the appointed warrior, rooted to the spot with fear, was slain and cut to pieces by the giant. The giant would then retreat, satisfied, into the dark forest. Over the years the little village had lost all its best men. The traveller was shocked by the story, and all the more shocked when he learned that this year he was the only man who could face the giant and save the women and children.

The next morning he found himself in the field where all the others had perished, waiting for the giant to appear from the forest. He did not have long to wait. The giant was more frightening than he had thought possible. He too felt himself rooted to the spot with fear. And then, by some instinct, he took one very small step towards the giant. He let out a gasp as he was sure something had happened when he stepped forward – but how could anything have happened? His heart thumping against his rib-cage, he took one more tiny step towards the giant and gasped again. Another step, and another. His steps got bigger as he got into his stride. And as he moved towards the giant, there was no doubt that the giant shrank a little with each step. By the time he was standing beside the giant, his sword poised for the kill, the giant was only the height of his knees. As he plunged the sword, he demanded, 'Who are you?'

The giant whispered with his last breath, 'Your fears.'

Adapted by the author from 'Giant Steps' in Parkin 1998

➤ 6 Round: 'A giant I once faced and beat was . . .'

Resources None.

Aim To discuss the challenges and fears pupils have faced in the past with regard to school work.

What to do The pupils sit in an inward-facing circle. In turn, they finish the sentence 'A giant I once faced and beat was . . .', naming an occasion when they were challenged but won through. The smallest victory counts.

SEEING IS BELIEVING!

After the round, ask each child how the challenge was met. What did they think, feel and do to be successful in beating the giant?

➤ 7 Round: 'A giant I am facing now is . . .'

Resources None.

Aim To encourage pupils to identify any study problems they would like help with.

What to do The pupils sit in an inward-facing circle. They raise their hand if they wish to speak. Invite them to identify a giant they are currently facing, finishing the sentence 'A giant I am facing now is . . .'. The other pupils can offer ideas to help them face the giant.

■ APPRAISAL

Encourage the pupils to start a collection of optical illusions. The following websites will help: www.amazing-optical-illusions.com; www.drawright.com

➤ The *RSG!* Round: Making 'I' contact

See Conversation 1 (page 29).

Seeing is Believing!

➤ Try these optical illusions.

Pixel Pete wants to keep the picture as he sees it the first time. But Katy Kite can explore other ways of seeing the pictures – if you let her!

Have a look at the illusions below. Can you 'swap' the way you view them and see both versions? Try to draw them yourself.

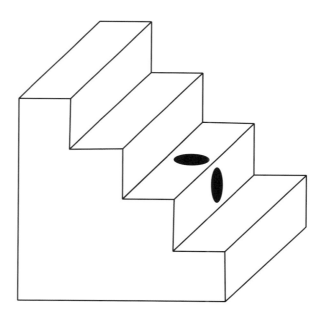

Questions

● What else that you know might be or is an illusion?

● What is real?

● Do we always see what's there or just some of it?

BACK IN THE MAGICAL MANSION

■ APPROACH

The second part of the story introduces the final two characters. The conversations that follow the story take the pupils through a now familiar exploration of the preferences and characteristics of these two new characters. The final message of the story is that it is best for all the friends to work together. We know from the research that 'deep' learners use head, hand and heart, not just the head. They also combine analytical and holistic approaches to learning to become versatile students.

■ ACTION

1 Read the second part of the story (Photocopiable 9.1, pages 75–76). Remind the pupils to visualise what they hear as strongly and in as much detail as they can.

2 Ask the pupils to complete the characters worksheet for this part of the story (Photocopiable 9.2, page 77). Try to avoid showing the children any of the illustrations of the two characters in the book at this stage.

3 Hand out 'The Magical Mansion Gang' worksheet (Photocopiable 9.3, page 78) and discuss the characters. To support you in building a more detailed understanding of the different characteristics of the last two members of the gang and to encourage discussion, see 'Key Characteristics' (Photocopiable 0.1, pages 14–15). This table may be used as a prompt for the pupils or as a resource to organise ideas for teaching.

■ APPRAISAL

You can choose to discuss the story while you tell it or after you tell it (or not). Often, leaving it 'in suspense' creates excitement for the next lesson.

➤ The *RSG!* Round: Making 'I' contact

Resources A copy of 'The Three H's Capture List 2' (Photocopiable 0.3, page 27) for each child.

Aim To capture thinking, doing and feeling responses after a session or series of sessions and to create empathy and further discussion on issues raised.

What to do The pupils sit in a circle and in turn answer the questions on 'The Three H's Capture List 2'. After the session they can write their conclusions on the worksheet.

In later conversations, the pupils use Photocopiables 0.2 and 0.3 as appropriate when carrying out this round.

Back in the Magical Mansion page 1

One day, Pixel Pete and Katy Kite met up with two other characters who lived in the Magical Mansion. They must have been in the Magical Mansion all the time, but Katy Kite and Pixel Pete had only caught glimpses of them before. The Magical Mansion was so big!

Their names were Handy Sam and Felix Hart. Let me tell you about them.

Handy Sam was cool. He took action when it was needed. He was very practical and loved to do things with his hands. Somehow or other, he always worked out what he needed, when he needed it and where, and he always had the right stuff to hand. He was good at doing things. That's why he was called Handy Sam. He loved to touch things and take them apart and put them together again, and he was fascinated by all sorts of materials.

Felix Hart, on the other hand, was less practical and more gentle. He could sometimes be unkind or hard on others (or himself), especially when he felt threatened, but generally he wanted life to go well for himself and others. He felt things quite deeply, although he didn't always say so.

Handy Sam's room in the Magical Mansion was like a workshop. There was a large bench with tools on it. There were several spotlights stored under the bench and a huge torch on the worktop. There were plans and charts pinned to the wall and manuals on a metal shelving unit. There were storage bins on a rack that held pens and pencils of all sorts, along with keys and plugs.

Felix Hart's room was quite different. A lava lamp by his bed gave a soft orange glow to the room. There were pictures of friends and family everywhere. A display case held pebbles, stones and bits of wood that he had picked up on his walks through the countryside around the mansion. He had some plants on the windowsill. There was a fish tank in a corner with some beautifully coloured fish swimming in the water. He had a lovely soft sofa and a table where he served drinks and biscuits.

The others realised, early on in their friendship, that how Felix was feeling about things tended to affect everybody. When he was happy, everyone was happy. When he was sad, his best friends felt sad too. They thought of him as the weather man – how he felt affected the atmosphere in the mansion and how the others felt. His friends had to think hard and do something to cheer him up. Sometimes, sensitive Felix would lose a bit of his confidence or feel tired and then it was quite difficult to get him to cheer up.

Back in the Magical Mansion page 2

Katy Kite, Pixel Pete and Handy Sam used all sorts of tricks to help Felix Hart feel better. Pixel Pete helped Felix think about how he was thinking, Katy Kite came up with creative ways to distract Felix, and Handy Sam would get everyone involved in a project. Often these tactics worked, and before long Felix Hart would be laughing and smiling and they would all go out and have fun.

Just like Katy Kite and Pixel Pete earlier, the friends found out that they got most done when they worked together. All of them were more clever together than one of them alone.

- On his own, Handy Sam would fidget a lot and not get much done.

- On his own, Felix Hart would have time to concentrate on his feelings and become a bit moody or worried.

- On her own, Katy Kite would get lost in her thoughts.

- On his own, Pixel Pete would get stuck into analysing something and forget his friends.

However, when they worked and played together, Handy Sam, Felix Hart, Katy Kite and Pixel Pete always had the best time and got the most done. When they realised this, even though they were quite different, they formed the strongest of bonds and became life-long friends.

The Characters Felix Hart and Handy Sam

➤ Draw the two new characters. Use the rest of the space to record your thoughts about Felix Hart and Handy Sam. You might want to think about what each of them looks like, their character, their strengths and how they like to do things.

Felix Hart

Handy Sam

The Magical Mansion Gang: Felix Hart and Handy Sam

➤ Handy Sam and Felix Hart are as different from one another as are Pixel Pete and Katy Kite.

Handy Sam
Gets things done.

A practical character with a particular genius for doing. He really is in touch with the world and is a great organiser.

He learns through action. He always wears his tool-belt so that he is ready to work.

Felix Hart
Feels his way.

Felix is probably the most influential character in the gang. He affects the actions of the others for much of the time. He is at the centre of every learning activity, just as the heart is at the centre of our chests, and he is often the gatekeeper to successful study for pupils, both young and old. The other characters need to pay attention to him and give him the opportunity to express his feelings and make them manageable.

THE CHARACTERS HANDY SAM AND FELIX HART

■ APPROACH

This conversation asks the pupils once again to visit the Magical Mansion and to think about and discuss the characters in the story. There is a sheet for them to record what they remember and think about Handy Sam and Felix Hart. This is not a memory test, but a record of what has struck them – a useful indication of their inner thinking.

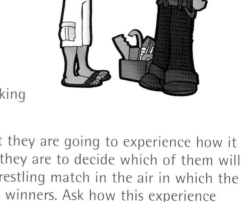

■ ACTION

➤ 1 Game: Arm Wrestle

Resources None.

Aim To help the pupils experience the advantage of working together to gain a win–win outcome.

What to do Ask the pupils to find a partner. Explain that they are going to experience how it feels to be a winner, and how it feels to be a loser. First they are to decide which of them will win the first game. Then ask them to perform an arm-wrestling match in the air in which the nominated person wins within 30 seconds. Celebrate the winners. Ask how this experience felt for the winner and the loser. Now repeat this with the same pair, with the other person winning within 30 seconds. Ask for feedback on that experience. Now ask them both to work together to win as many times as they can in 30 seconds.

➤ 2 Discussion

Ask for thoughts on the last game. What was the message of the game? How is it linked with Handy Sam and Felix Hart? Remind them if necessary that Handy Sam and Felix Hart are friends.

➤ 3 Activities

Discuss the preferences and characteristics of Handy Sam and Felix Hart before completing the worksheets (Photocopiables 10.1, 10.2 and 10.3, pages 81–83). Value the ideas they produce and congratulate them on their thinking. There are no right and wrong answers in terms of what they think – because that's what they think. It is this thinking that you want to get a picture of in order to explore their approach to study.

- Ask the pupils to complete the task individually, entering a few key words or ideas to make lists on Photocopiable 10.1.

- Ask them to talk these through with a partner and share their ideas.

- Now, in groups of four, ask them to come up with some ideas about why these characteristics are strengths. They should write their answers in the boxes on Photocopiables 10.2 and 10.3. What would people with these qualities do for their friends? What advantages would there be in knowing them?

- Take feedback from the class.

- You could complete each character's page together on a whiteboard or flipchart and then discuss your findings, especially the strengths.

THE CHARACTERS HANDY SAM AND FELIX HART

■ APPRAISAL

➤ 1 Round: 'I like . . . '

Resources None.

Aim To help pupils start to think about and appreciate the differences between the characters of Handy Sam and Felix Hart.

What to do Each child chooses one of the characters. In turn, they pretend to be the character they have chosen. Ask them to finish the sentence 'I like . . .'. They can say favourite food, hobby or item of clothing, but not people. The other pupils put their hand up after each turn if they also like the same thing.

➤ 2 The *RSG!* Round: Making 'I' contact

See Conversation 9 (page 74).

➤ 3 The *RSG!* Gang Help Round

Resources None.

Aim To reflect on how the characters could help pupils tackle a particular challenge or learning task.

What to do The pupils sit in a circle facing each other. Taking the role of each character for a single round, they complete the following sentences:

'Handy Sam would help me by . . . '

'Pixel Pete would help me by . . . '

'Felix Hart would help me by . . . '

'Katy Kite would help me by . . . '

Handy Sam's and Felix Hart's Characteristics

➤ Let's get to know Handy Sam and Felix Hart!

Write down things that describe Handy Sam's character:

Write down things that describe Felix Hart's character:

**Now, think again: which character are you more like?
(draw an X on the line)**

Handy Sam ——————————————————————————————— **Felix Hart**

Handy Sam: Someone who Gets Things Done

➤ Do you know someone who is really good with their hands – at taking action?

If you can't think of someone you know, then think of a comic, cartoon, film or TV character – even an animal – who makes you think of Handy Sam.

● How do you know they are like Handy Sam? What do they do and say that makes you think they are a strong, handy thinker? Write a few ideas in the box below.

● Now, think very carefully. Why are these characteristics *strengths*?

● Discuss your ideas with someone else and write down some new ideas.

● Record all the things you have found out in class about your friends and characters who are like Handy Sam.

Felix Hart: Someone who Manages their Feelings

➤ Do you know someone who is really good at understanding feelings?

  If you can't think of someone you know, then think of a comic, cartoon, film or TV character – even an animal – who makes you think of Felix Hart.

● How do you know they are like Felix? What do they do and say that makes you think they are strong, heart-felt thinkers? Write a few ideas in the box below:

● Now, think very carefully. Why are these characteristics *strengths*?

● Discuss your ideas with someone else and write down some new ideas.

● Record all the things you have found out in class about your friends and characters who are like Felix Hart.

CELEBRATING STRENGTHS

■ APPROACH

This conversation prompts the pupils to consider all four characters from the Magical Mansion Gang and asks them to discuss what they have discovered about the strengths of each. This helps them to develop further understanding about themselves and others and about the role of diversity in providing strengths and not perceived weaknesses.

■ ACTION

➤ 1 Game: Pass a Smile

Resources None.

Aim To establish eye contact and create a positive atmosphere.

What to do Ask someone to start by passing a smile to their neighbour. The smile is passed round everyone until all are smiling.

➤ 2 Game: The Name Game

Resources Beanbag.

Aim Fun, warming-up exercise.

What to do The pupils stand in an inward-facing circle. The first pupil calls out the name of another pupil in the circle, and gently throws a beanbag. If the recipient catches it, they throw it to someone else. If not, the first child throws it to another child. After throwing the beanbag successfully, the child sits down. The game continues until all the pupils are sitting down.

➤ 3 Describing the Magical Mansion Gang

Ask the pupils to consider all of the Magical Mansion Gang. Encourage them to share their thinking about the different characteristics of Pixel Pete, Katy Kite, Handy Sam and Felix Hart with others in the class and to think about the strengths of other pupils. They can work on this individually or in groups, or you may prefer to take feedback from the whole class, ensuring that they all have an understanding of the qualities of each character. A worksheet is provided to record their thoughts on (see column 1 of Photocopiable 11.1, page 86). Alternatively, you could read out the list of strengths that follows and ask the pupils to work out which description of strengths fits which character.

CELEBRATING STRENGTHS

Who am I?

> Is really good with practical things, being organised, getting things done, can take things apart and put them together again, understands how things work, is good at technology, and sport?
> (Handy Sam)

> Doesn't lose things, likes everything to be in order, likes science and maths amongst other subjects?
> (Pixel Pete)

> Is really good to their friends, thinks about how they are, can see how things are going for them, is gentle and caring, may become frightened, sometimes loses heart and needs encouragement and safety and friends?
> (Felix Hart)

> Is really creative, loves art and music, and fairy tales and magic, and is quiet and reflective?
> (Katy Kite)

■ APPRAISAL

Now that we have met all of the Magical Mansion Gang, we can begin to think about how they can help us in studying by giving us strength when we need it.

➤ Round: 'I was strong when . . . '

Resources None.

Aim To discuss the strengths pupils have used in the past.

What to do The pupils sit in an inward-facing circle. In turn they finish the sentence 'I was strong when . . . ', naming an occasion when they found their own strength.

Ask each child how this happened. What did they think, feel and do to be strong? Were they strong on their own or did they call for help? What happened?

After this, ask the children to complete the second column of the worksheet 'What Strengths Have we Found?' (Photocopiable 11.1, page 86).

➤ The *RSG!* Round: Making 'I' contact

See Conversation 9 (page 74).

What Strengths Have we Found?

	List their strengths	How I could be more like . . .
Pixel Pete		
Katy Kite		
Handy Sam		
Felix Hart		

X MARKS THE SPOT!

■ APPROACH

Conversation 12 represents a key point in the unfolding journey of development. The pupils are asked to plot their own characteristics and study preferences on a series of lines to find out where their strengths lie, as represented by the four characters of the Magical Mansion Gang.

- This conversation may be linked to the evaluation aspect of STRIDE: finding the value in self (see Conversation 4).

■ ACTION

➤ 1 Game: Pass a Wave

Resources None.

Aim To generate a sense of co-operation.

What to do All stand in a circle. Begin the session by greeting one another. Then wave to the pupil on your right. Ask the children to pass the wave on round the circle until it comes back to you.

➤ 2 Game: We're all Different

Resources None.

Aim To remind each pupil that they are unique.

What to do The pupils sit in a circle. Call out a category. All the pupils who are within that category stand and move to a new place in the circle. Examples of categories are pupils who have kept trying with a hard piece of work, pupils who have done some good work in the last week, pupils who have brought their PE kit today, and pupils who completed their homework last night. You could invite the children to think of other categories to do with study.

➤ 3 Self- and peer-evaluation

The exercises provide stimulus and information for discussion with a partner, moving around different partners, working in small groups and providing feedback, explanations and insights to each other and with you. This is an opportunity to allow every child to feel valued at a point in the journey where they have learned about themselves and received positive feedback from peers and teacher.

On the worksheet 'Let's Think about You' (Photocopiable 12.1, page 90), the pupils are asked to place themselves on a line in relation to each character.

Explain to them that an X placed on the line close to 'Not much' is not like a low score. They are building up a picture of their strengths and areas to develop as they get older. This is all about growth over time and positive possibilities. This is a snapshot of their thinking, not a limiting exercise. It is a prompt for further discussion and development of their internal perceptions of the world, themselves and others.

X MARKS THE SPOT!

- The pupils work together to build up their profile of characteristics and strengths and present it as a visual tool in quadrants. A worksheet (Photocopiable 12.2, page 91) is supplied, and a completed example is below. Asking other pupils for their points of view increases each child's awareness of and empathy with the others. It also helps them to clarify their own characteristics in their own mind each time they make a decision about someone else. This is the point when pupils begin to build up the whole picture of where they are individually in terms of the different learning behaviours they have been discussing. They transfer their individual lines onto the large cross and add a photo.

- They then join up their X marks to form a shape that they can colour in. This visual tool represents the pattern of their characteristics as they see them (with help from their friends) at this stage in their school life.

A completed chart

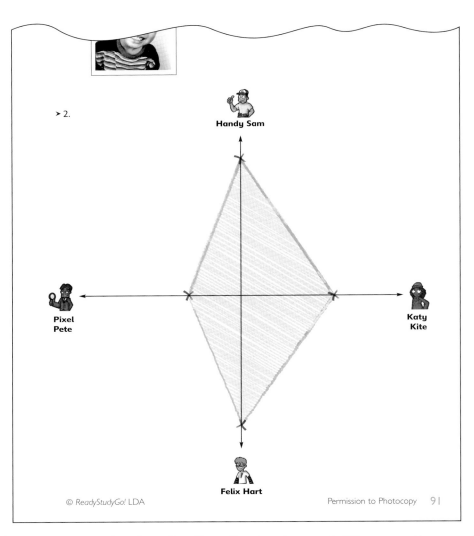

Permission to Photocopy   91

Think of this as a compass showing directions for development. Where are they coming from? Where do they need to go? Where do their strengths lie? Where can they get stronger? There is no set pattern.

You can repeat this activity each term, so that the pupils can assess any changes.

X MARKS THE SPOT!

■ APPRAISAL

Display each pupil's chart in the classroom together with their 'Inside my own Magical Mansion' drawings from earlier (see Conversation 2).

Using their understanding of the four characters, the characteristics pages and their compass chart, pupils can produce a summary page of what they have found out that is good about themselves and record their findings on the worksheet provided (Photocopiable 12.3, page 92).

➤ Round: 'I am like . . . [Pixel Pete, Felix Hart, Handy Sam or Katy Kite] because . . . '

Resources None.

Aim To explore themselves in relation to the story characters.

What to do The pupils think of some things that have helped them locate themselves on the lines for the chart. In turn, they complete the sentence 'I am like . . . [Pixel Pete, Felix Hart, Handy Sam or Katy Kite] because . . .'.

➤ The *RSG!* Round: Making 'I' contact

See Conversation 9 (page 74).

➤ Extension work

ICT

The pupils can transfer their charts to Microsoft Excel using the chart/radars function. They will need to think carefully about what scales to use on their chart.

➤ Group work

- Group together in fours those pupils who show similar patterns of characteristics and strengths and ask them to discuss and record some key points about how they approach homework. Ask them to reflect on what they noticed about the conversation. Sample questions for 'single characteristic' and 'mixed character' groups are provided on the worksheet 'How Do you . . .?' (Photocopiable 12.4, page 93). The pupils should keep a record of what they find out about their group.

- Now ask them to share in mixed groups and repeat the exercise.

- You can also explore other combined groupings in the class so that you seat the pupils in 'similar' or 'mixed' groupings and ask them to reflect on group performance for different tasks.

- Working in groups of four, place your other group members where you think they should be on the chart. See where they would put themselves. Discuss differences (as strengths). Then change the groups round.

Let's Think about You!

➤ You have now thought a lot about your four new friends from the Magical Mansion, their preferences, characteristics and personalities. Having done all that thinking, how much do you think you are like each character now?

Draw an X on the line to show how close you feel to each character.

How much like Pixel Pete are you?

Not much   **A lot**

●——●

How much like Katy Kite are you?

Not much   **A lot**

●——●

How much like Felix Hart are you?

Not much   **A lot**

●——●

How much like Handy Sam are you?

Not much   **A lot**

●——●

(12.2)

Two Pictures of Me

➤ 1.

┌─────────────────┐
│   │
│   Stick   │
│ photograph   │
│   here   │
│   │
│   │
└─────────────────┘

Handy Sam

➤ 2.

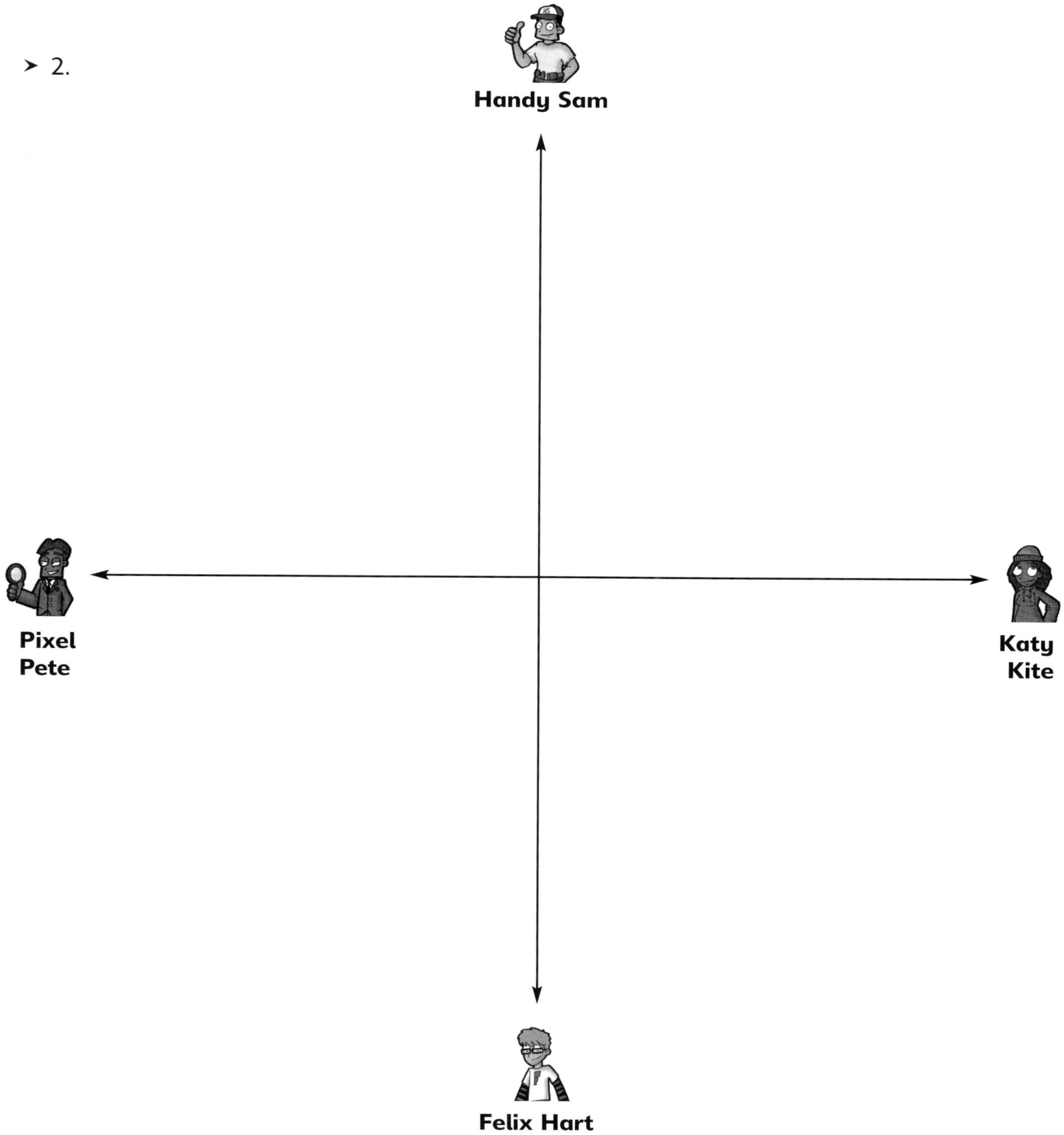

**Pixel
Pete**

**Katy
Kite**

Felix Hart

All that's Good about Myself

➤ Make a list of all the good things that you have found out about yourself.

Use these strong characteristics when you study! Keep this list nearby to remind yourself how you study effectively.

© *ReadyStudyGo!* LDA   Permission to Photocopy

How Do you . . .?

➤ Here are some questions to ask in your groups. Use them to find out how others react in situations. Use the back to devise some questions of your own to answer in your groups.

How do you...	Pupil 1	Pupil 2	Pupil 3	Pupil 4
pack your school bag?				
read a book?				
tidy your room?				
react to a success?				
react to being praised?				
think about the future?				
find your way round a place you haven't been to before?				
watch TV – what kinds of programmes do you like?				

OUR CLASS

■ APPROACH

Through this conversation, the pupils can see where everyone is in a bigger picture of preferences, characteristics and strengths, all of which have a part to play in how they approach study. They can reflect on their own qualities as a group and how they are looking after each other as a class in terms of studying.

- Like Conversation 12, this conversation may be linked to the evaluation aspect of STRIDE – finding the value in self (Conversation 4).

■ ACTION

➤ 1 Game: All Change

Resources Category cards (optional).

Aim To mix the pupils up, have fun.

What to do The pupils sit in an inward-facing circle. Either you or a child calls out different categories (these could be on cards). All the pupils who fit into that category have to change seats. Examples of categories: anyone with black hair, a birthday in September, or a pet hamster.

➤ 2 Class chart

- Make a very large version of the compass chart so that everyone's name can be fitted on it on small name cards or sticky notes (see Photocopiable 12.2, page 91).

- Make a rule suggesting that if the pupil is closer than half-way along a line to the character, they can put their name on the class chart close to that character. If this produces too many pupils in several categories, then ask for those who are three-quarters or more along the line towards the character to put their name on the chart.

- Ask the pupils to come up and put themselves in the place where they show the strongest preferences, characteristics and strengths. This might be close to Katy Kite for example; or, if a child has found themselves to be quite like Felix Hart and Pixel Pete, they can stick their name near both. Some pupils may be very clearly in one place; others may have two, three or four cards on the chart showing where their strengths lie. Ask the pupils to talk about their placement(s).

- Make the link back to study very clear. Their wide range of strengths, both individually and as a group, can help each child study better and they can help each other to study better. Knowing the class preferences, characteristics and strengths makes a strong resource for the pupils to call upon for help. Asking for help is a key study skill, especially if they know that they can hear the suggestions of their peers without judgement.

- The pupils can call on their peers who have particular strengths in certain areas. Similarly, the pupils can be encouraged to help others in their study.

OUR CLASS

➤ 3 Experts

Start a conversation in which pupils can bring specific difficulties they are experiencing to the class and the experts with specific preferences can sit together and offer advice.

➤ 4 Magical Mansion Gang members

As a variation on this, encourage them to use the members of the Magical Mansion Gang to help them imagine different world views. Ask them to suggest solutions to study issues and problems from their point of view; for example, 'Bethany, what would Handy Sam suggest here?'

➤ 5 Props

Use props to represent each character – for example, a glove for Handy Sam, a heart badge (or an armband with a heart on it) for Felix Hart, a magnifying glass for Pixel Pete and a hat for Katy Kite. The pupils can think up some other props.

➤ 6 Game: To the Rescue!

Resources Written prompts.

Aim To explore the characteristics of the four friends in the story in relation to solving study problems.

What to do The pupils stand in an inward-facing circle. They are given one of four colours in turn, each colour representing one of Handy Sam, Pixel Pete, Katy Kite and Felix Hart. A folded piece of paper is placed in the centre of the circle. On it is written one of the following prompts:

- an aspect of study life – for example, homework, revision, groupwork, research, library;

- a study scenario – for example, 'You have run out of time for . . . ', 'You have a test in three days but your friends want you to play football tonight.'

You could invite the pupils to suggest issues for the folded paper in the centre of the circle.

Call out any of the four colours. All the pupils in that category run in a clockwise direction around the outside of the circle. When they reach their places again, they may enter the circle to pick up the paper in the centre. Whoever picks up the paper has to explain how their character would react to the situation. The others who have the same colour say if they agree or would do something different. Capture the different responses for discussion later. Then either call a new colour or replace the paper with a new prompt.

To add fun, call 'To the rescue' while the pupils are running round. Then they have to change direction and run round the circle anti-clockwise.

➤ 7 Game: Get Sticking!

This game asks pupils to decide where they would put their friend on the compass chart (Photocopiable 13.1, page 98). Using name cards or removable stickers, they position their friends and peers.

OUR CLASS

➤ 8 Guiding their behaviour

You can point out areas they need to concentrate on for different topic work. For instance, 'We need a lot more Pixel Pete thinking here . . . ', 'I want you to think much more about what Felix would say about this historical character.' The compass chart can alert the pupils to where they need to be in terms of the work being done. A history lesson that involves empathy will have Felix Hart to the fore. A practical lesson will feature Handy Sam.

The charts also provide a resource if the pupils' approach is inappropriate for study. Refer back to the fact that Pixel Pete, Katy Kite, Handy Sam and Felix Hart achieved the best results when they worked together. You could refer to different aspects of an optical illusion, which is stronger as a whole (see Conversation 8).

➤ 9 Locating subjects on the compass chart

Practical subjects will have them working in the northern hemisphere, maths and science in the north-west, arts in the east and south. You could use Photocopiable 13.1 on page 98 to chart the subjects they are studying together (see the example below that indicates one interpretation). The stereotypical responses to the nature of topics are not necessarily true. Imaginative thinking and emotional engagement belong just as much to maths and science as they do to more overtly south-east quadrant topics.

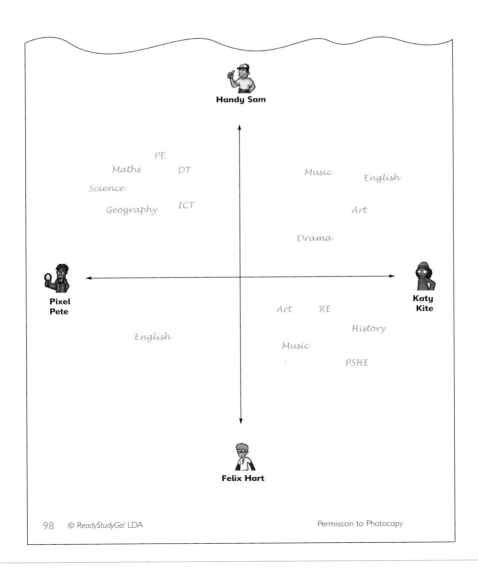

OUR CLASS

■ APPRAISAL

➤ Game: Problem Solving at the Magical Mansion

Aim To encourage role play as all four characters in order to solve real issues.

What to do The pupils are divided into groups of four. Each group represents the Magical Mansion Gang. Each group is given a problem which they have to solve, with every member of the group playing a part. The following are suggested problems to get them started – but ideally you should use study problems submitted by the pupils in advance.

- I have lost my bag.

- I haven't done last night's homework because there was no time.

- I'm really worried about a class test in English next week.

- I've moved house and have a new bedroom and want to work out how to set it up for work and play.

A variation is to use homogeneous groups. Then the problems are solved by, for example, a group of Handy Sams. This will provide more than one solution from that point of view.

➤ The *RSG!* Round: Making 'I' contact

See Conversation 9 (page 74).

Our Class's Characteristics and Strengths

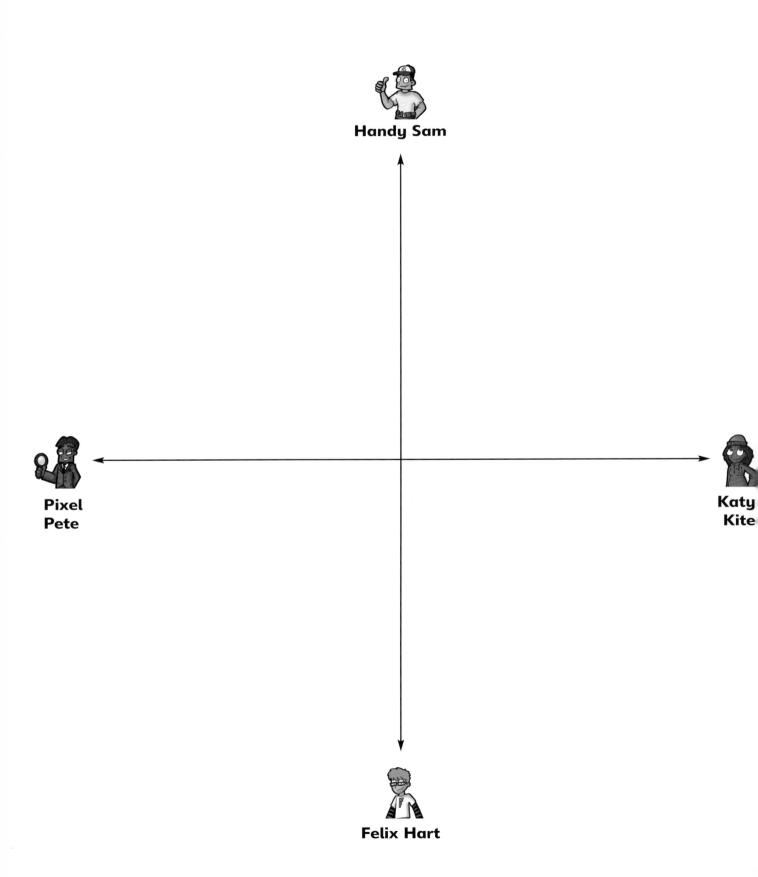

MIRROR, MIRROR

■ APPROACH

In this conversation, the pupils are asked to think about what they have learned since the beginning of the course. This is not a memory exercise or test. The aim is to support the transition to the next stage of their journey, whatever that might be – a new teacher, a new year, a new school.

■ ACTION

➤ 1 Game: Mirror Image

Resources None.

Aim To work with someone who is not a close friend.

What to do The pupils are divided into pairs (A and B) and stand facing each other. B is to be the mirror image of A. Tell the A's that their partner is going to follow their actions as if they are their reflection. Ask the A's to start slowly and speed up when the B's become more confident. Reverse roles after a couple of minutes.

➤ 2 Reflecting on what we have learned

Ask the pupils to complete the worksheet 'Reflection Time' (Photocopiable 14.1, page 100). Be open to their thinking, whatever it is. Allow them to feel safe in venturing what they really think. Value their reflections.

➤ 3 Think back to Conversation 3 'What is Study?'

Discuss and record how their thinking has developed since the opening stages of the journey.

➤ 4 Review the STRIDE mnemonic in Conversation 4 'In your Stride!'

Where are they on their journey? What have they learned about themselves and others, about how they and others learn, about strengths in different characteristics and team building? How would each of the four characters respond to each of the prompts in the mnemonic?

➤ 5 Review their strengths as a class

Recall the findings of Conversation 13. You could use the worksheet 'What Strengths have we Found?' (Photocopiable 14.2, page 101).

■ APPRAISAL

Provide feedback for each pupil using stickers and certificates (a certificate is supplied as Photocopiable 14.3, page 102).

➤ The *RSG!* Round: Making 'I' contact

See Conversation 9 (page 74).

Reflection Time

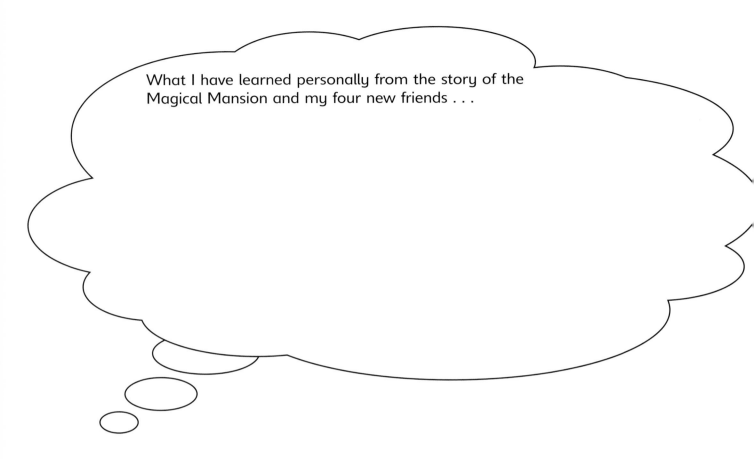

What I have learned personally from the story of the Magical Mansion and my four new friends . . .

What have I learned about myself as a student? (Write findings in the box below.)

What Strengths Have we Found?

➤ Use this chart to find a person to help you.

	Who is good at . . .
Starting S	
Teaching T	
Reflection R	
Imagination I	
Discussion D	
Evaluation E	

Certificate of Achievement

Presented to

_____

For

_____

_____

_____

_____

_____

By

_____

WHERE TO NEXT?

■ APPROACH

The final conversations in the course begin to set up the thinking for the rest of the journey. Some of the pupils will be going on to the next stage of schooling. It may be daunting to face change and the unknown. If appropriate, you may be able to work these sessions into the existing transition arrangements operated by your school both for internal and external transfer and for induction.

Re-read the story of the Young Hero and the Giant in Conversation 8 (page 71). This conversation is designed to bring to the surface any issues and fears the pupils may have at the back of their minds so that the fears, like the giant, will reduce in size as they take steps towards them. They can also gain advice from their peers.

■ ACTION

Let's think through some of the challenges and fears.

➤ 1 Questions

The pupils work in pairs to answer these questions:

- What do you think it is going to be like in your new situation?

- Do you know any children who are there already?

- If 'Yes', what do they say about it? How has it been for them?

➤ 2 Discussion

- What obstacles are going to be in your way in the near future?

- Can you say what they are?

- Are they real or imagined?

- How serious are they?

- Are the obstacles we face the same for lots of us?

- Whom can you ask for help?

- Which of the Magical Mansion Gang will be of most help to you?

- Can someone suggest some ways round the obstacles?

Summarise the findings of the discussion, pointing out any strategies the pupils agree on and any useful pointers that emerge.

WHERE TO NEXT?

■ APPRAISAL

The pupils will have to learn to adapt to new situations as they move on in their journey, to trust new friends if they move class or school, and to trust new teachers.

➤ The *RSG!* Round: Making 'I' contact

See Conversation 9 (page 74).

➤ Game: Pass It On

Resources None.

Aim To establish eye contact and finish on an 'up'.

What to do Ask the children to stand and make a thumbs-up gesture with their left hand. Either start yourself or invite a pupil to start. Begin by turning to the person on your left and give them a thumbs-up. They then repeat this, passing the movement round the circle until it gets back to you.

ADVICE FOR THE FUTURE FROM THE MAGICAL MANSION GANG

■ APPROACH

As the Magical Mansion Gang get ready to say goodbye for now, the pupils gather the advice the characters would give. The pupils revisit the STRIDE mnemonic from Conversation 4 and the advice each member of the gang would give is recorded for each 'footstep'.

■ ACTION

➤ 1 Group work

The pupils form into groups of four. If possible, two groups should be working on each of the four advice worksheets (Photocopiables 16.1 to 16.4, pages 107–110); these can be photocopied in different colours. Ask each group to be the character on their sheet, to brainstorm some advice to add to the advice already given for each footstep in STRIDE (see pages 51–57) and to discuss the information on each sheet.

They then go to the other group working on the same character and add to their own sheet, building up a resource of suggestions.

You could continue this activity by giving each group a new character until all the children have advice from each of the four characters.

➤ 2 Discussion

The groups then swap ideas and get ready for the final whole-class session.

➤ 3 The *RSG!* Round: Making 'I' contact

See Conversation 9 (page 74).

➤ 4 Whole-class session

The pupils gather together their worksheets, drawings and other resources created during the course. They bring them to a final session in the studio. Ask each one of them in turn to complete the following:

- 'My high was . . . ' and 'My low was . . . '.
- 'What I changed most in my thinking about study and school was . . . '.
- 'What I changed most in doing study and school was . . . '.
- 'What I changed most in my feelings about study and school was . . . '.
- 'I am looking forward most to . . . '.

Let the pupils all complete the first sentence, then the second and so on.

Before you end the session, give out 'Some More Wisdom from the Magical Mansion Gang' (Photocopiable 16.5, page 111).

This is the final opportunity for classmates to offer any help. The session closes with the hand chase game.

ADVICE FOR THE FUTURE FROM THE MAGICAL MANSION GANG

➤ 5 Game: Hand Chase

Resources Tables and chairs.

Aim Fun, concentration, co-operation, friendship, confidence.

What to do Arrange the tables as a large central 'boardroom' – with everyone sitting around the edge with no gaps. Put your left hand on the table and ask the pupils to do the same. Put your right hand over the top of the left arm of the child who is sitting on your right, making sure that both your right hand and the child's left hand are side by side, with the arms crossed but not touching. The class follows suit and a circle of hands is now laid out on the table.

Decide whether you are starting in a clockwise or anticlockwise direction. Raise your right hand without lifting your wrist and gently tap the table once. That tap now has to continue as an unbroken pattern of taps made by the hands that are side by side, right round the table in the agreed direction. This means that you sometimes have to tap with your left hand and sometimes with your right, going in an anticlockwise direction. Once the person to your left has tapped, you then have to wait for the person on your right to tap their left hand (as it is the next hand in the sequence) before you tap your right, even though the temptation is to tap next. The tap goes slowly round the table. The idea is to make this as smooth and rhythmic as possible.

Variation 1

If a child accidentally taps with the wrong hand or the wrong person taps with either hand, they have lost a life for that hand. Next time they tap with the wrong hand they have to remove that hand. (You can play 'one false tap and you're out' when the pupils have practised and become more proficient.) The last person left in wins.

Variation 2

When the tap comes back to you, you can send it round again or change the direction by tapping twice. Pupils can change the direction too.

▪ ACCLAMATION

It is good to mark the end of the course with music or a classroom party or picnic. The pupils can choose their favourite games. All around them on the walls of the classroom is their work: their heads, their characteristics, preferences and strengths, their compass charts, and so on, to remind them to be their best as students.

Advice from Handy Sam for your Next Steps

Here's some advice to help you next time!

Starting	**S**	
Teaching self	**T**	
Reflection	**R**	
Imagination	**I**	
Discussion	**D**	
Evaluation	**E**	

Advice from Pixel Pete for your Next Steps

	Here's some advice to help you next time!
● **Starting** **S**	
● **Teaching self** **T**	
● **Reflection** **R**	
● **Imagination** **I**	
● **Discussion** **D**	
● **Evaluation** **E**	

16.3

Advice from Katy Kite for your Next Steps

	Here's some advice to help you next time!
Starting **S**	
Teaching self **T**	
Reflection **R**	
Imagination **I**	
Discussion **D**	
Evaluation **E**	

Advice from Felix Hart for your Next Steps

	Here's some advice to help you next time!
Starting **S**	
Teaching self **T**	
Reflection **R**	
Imagination **I**	
Discussion **D**	
Evaluation **E**	

Some More Wisdom from the Magical Mansion Gang

➤ Expect difficulty. Don't be put off by it. Treat it as a challenge.

➤ Aim for your personal best.

➤ Think like a champion athlete when tackling your studies.

➤ Surprise, surprise, you are not a perfect student or an exam-seeking missile (are you?), but you can get better at it, you can do better. Go for your best.

➤ Grow into an independent student. It is a skill that will last you for life in study at school and college, and in work.

➤ Think of yourself as self-employed and of study as your business. The more effort you put in to building your 'business' success, the more 'profit' you will make. The less you attend to your business, the more likely it is that you will make a loss. You know which option makes sense for you and your life.